CARL SANDBURG'S AMERICA

A Study of His Works, His Politics,
and His New Imagination

First Edition

By Evert Villarreal

cognella®
academic publishing

Bassim Hamadeh, CEO and Publisher
Michael Simpson, Vice President of Acquisitions
Jamie Giganti, Managing Editor
Jess Busch, Senior Graphic Designer
Marissa Applegate, Acquisitions Editor
Brian Fahey, Licensing Specialist
Sean Adams, Interior Design

First published in the United States of America in 2015 by Cognella, Inc.

Cover image copyright © Al Ravenna / New York World-Telegram & Sun / Public Domain.

Printed in the United States of America.

ISBN: 978-1-63189-209-7 (pbk) / 978-1-63189-210-3 (br)

www.cognella.com   800-200-3908

Contents

For Isabel, my beautiful, brilliant, and wonderful wife. She is my muse!

For Matthew, Thomas, and Luke, our sons.
They are the inspiration and motivation for everything I do in life.

To my parents, Sabas and Betty Villarreal, who have taught me the value of hard work and have given me the gift of optimism. They have always insisted that my life reflect a continuous journey to excellence, with no excuses. They are also the very people Carl Sandburg championed all of his life.

To my brother, Edgar Villarreal, who has always supported my professional career and is always there to lend a hand.

Finally, to my students, who have taught me so much over the last twenty years of college instruction.

No one will get at my verses who insists on
viewing them as a literary performance.

—Walt Whitman (from "A Backward Glance")

You ask me to belong to something. You wish me to join a movement
or party or church and subscribe to a creed and a program. It would
be easy to do this. It is the line of least resistance. If I have a fixed,
unchangeable creed then I am saved the trouble every day of forming a
new creed dictated by the events of the day. If I have a program and a
philosophy and a doctrine, crystalyzed [sic] in an organized movement,
then the movement is supposed to do for me what I ought to do for
myself.

—Letter from Carl Sandburg to Romain Rolland
(October, 1919) reprinted in Herbert
Mitgang's *The Letters of Carl Sandburg*

Introduction

C arl Sandburg was one of the most famous, beloved, and successful liter-
ary figures of the twentieth century. Between his birth in 1878 and his
death in 1967, he lived out an extremely productive, dynamic, and experimental
literary life.

Significant highlights in Carl Sandburg's career include winning the Helen
Haire Levinson Prize for best poems of the year in 1914; sharing the Poetry
Society of America Prize with Margaret Widdemer for *Cornhuskers* in 1919;
sharing the Poetry Society of America Annual Book Award with Stephen
Vincent Benét in 1921; reading as Phi Beta Kappa poet at Harvard in 1928;
being awarded the Order of the North Star by the King of Sweden in 1938;
winning the Pulitzer Prize in History in 1940 for *Abraham Lincoln: The War
Years*; being elected to the American Academy of Arts and Letters in 1940;
receiving the Pulitzer Prize in Poetry in 1951 for *Complete Poems*; receiving the
American Academy of Arts and Letters gold medal for history and biography
in 1952; receiving the Poetry Society of America gold medal in 1953; receiving
a citation from the U.S. Chamber of Commerce as Great Living American "for
lasting contribution to American literature" (Mitgang xiv). In addition, his novel
Remembrance Rock was a finalist for the Pulitzer Prize in Fiction in 1949—the
same year that Arthur Miller won the Pulitzer Prize for Drama for *Death of A
Salesman*.

Another highlight in his career includes the address he delivered before a Joint
Session of Congress on February 12, 1959—a date he fit into his busy schedule
that year—to commemorate the sesquicentennial of Abraham Lincoln's birth.

Although this address may not seem significant to some readers, it is important to note that Carl Sandburg has been *the only private citizen in American history* to address a Joint Session of Congress along with George Bancroft, the historian, who spoke to Congress "following the assassination of Lincoln" (Callahan 222). Also, on March 4, 1961, he spoke to a group of over 20,000 people on the east front of the United States Capitol to deliver another speech on Lincoln, this one commemorating the one-hundred-year anniversary of Lincoln's First Inaugural Address. It is also important to note that many Lincoln scholars would concede that Carl Sandburg's historical writings on Lincoln were extremely important in Abraham Lincoln's continuing popularity in the twentieth century. If this list of accolades and accomplishments is not enough, Carl Sandburg was also asked to write the Foreword to John F. Kennedy's 1962 book titled *To Turn the Tide*.

Long before Carl Sandburg appeared on the *Ed Sullivan Show* and on the *Milton Berle Show*, he had performed on almost every major college campus in the country, reading his poems, discussing current events, and talking about Abraham Lincoln. Also during his career he recorded many LPs of songs he loved and often performed as he traveled the country. In addition, he wrote hundreds of Forewards and Prefaces for the works of contemporaries he admired, and even wrote Prefaces for volumes of the collected works of Mark Twain and Walt Whitman, a poet whose work Carl Sandburg championed.

To give readers an additional sense of the level of Carl Sandburg's fame, on October 27, 1972—five years after Carl Sandburg's death—his home in Flat Rock, North Carolina, called Connemara, was dedicated as a national park and the home was officially designated a national historic site. About the designation and honor, Lauren Goff said that Carl Sandburg "became the first writer in the history of our nation whose home was made a national historic site by the federal government. Only presidents' homes were so designated before that. The second writer to be honored that way was Longfellow two years later, in 1974" (Swank 96).

Carl Sandburg's books often appeared on best seller lists. After *Chicago Poems* appeared in 1916, he published over thirty separate books. They consist of eight volumes of poetry; two separate multi-volume biographies of Abraham Lincoln (which, altogether total six volumes and more than 4,000 pages); a juvenile biography of Abraham Lincoln (the first of its kind); a biography of Edward Steichen (which was, at the time, the first biography of a photographer); a biography of Mary Todd Lincoln (one of the earliest biographies published about her life); a biography of Oliver R. Barrett—a man who spent more than fifty years assembling the most extensive, diverse, and important collections of publications about Abraham Lincoln; eleven very well-selling children's books; a very original book of American folk songs; one novel (which runs over 1,200 pages, and aims to retell American history); and an autobiography.

The major books that have appeared on Sandburg since 1990 include Penelope Niven's official biography of Sandburg titled *Carl Sandburg* (1991) [published by Scribner's], Philip Yannella's *The Other Carl Sandburg* (1996) [published by University Press of Mississippi], and Kenneth Dodson's *The Poet and the Sailor: The Story of My Friendship With Carl Sandburg* (2007) [published by University of Illinois Press]. All three books, especially the books by Niven and Yannella, are invaluable, adding immensely to Sandburg scholarship.

Other recent books and articles discuss Sandburg as well. For example, Joseph Thomas Jr.'s *Poetry's Playground: The Culture of Contemporary American Children's Poet* (2007) [published by Wayne State University Press] discusses Sandburg's popularity and his role in the development of children's books, and critical articles like John Marsh's "A Lost Art of Work: The Arts and Crafts Movement in Carl Sandburg's *Chicago Poems*" have appeared recently in *American Literature: A Journal of Literary History, Criticism, and Bibliography*.

Though critical interest in Carl Sandburg seems to be growing, what has appeared in the last decade focuses, for the most part, on his early works (or exclusively on *The People, Yes* [1936]). For example, J. G. Johansen's "They Will Say" (2001) takes a close look at this single poem that appears in *Chicago Poems*. Joseph Epstein's "The People's Poet" (1991) focused on an analysis of *Chicago Poems*; so does Mark Van Wienen's "Taming the Socialist: Carl Sandburg's *Chicago Poems* and Its Critics" (1991), published in *American Literature: A Journal of Literary History, Criticism, and Bibliography*.

The few publications that look at post-1920 works do reveal an interest in aspects of Carl Sandburg that are not political, and these articles are paving the way for a reassessment of Sandburg's works. Notable publications include J. D. Arenstein's essay "Carl Sandburg's Biblical Roots" (2003), which argues that *The People, Yes* "is not limited to expressing the conditions of its specific time and place—rather, it is shot through with biblical source material, analogues, and allusions" (Arenstein 54). Sally Greene's "'Things Money Cannot Buy': Carl Sandburg's Tribute to Virginia Woolf" (2001), published in the *Journal of Modern Literature*, begins by describing Sandburg's politics but ultimately explores how in 1941 "the quiet suicide of Virginia Woolf gave Carl Sandburg pause. For one moment, core questions about who he was, what he had once stood for, cast a shadow in his heart" (Greene 308). Greene's article ultimately describes a man who had, by 1941, practiced "self-censorship" and "put some distance between his position [regarding World War II] and Woolf's" (Greene 306).

After 1920, Carl Sandburg's political ideology and imagination grew in scope, breadth, and complexity, though it remained somewhat consistent with its pre-1920 Leftist origins. But the point to be underscored is that always at the center of Sandburg's concerns was the "common man" and the "working people"—interchangeable terms representing the group of Americans that Sandburg wanted to serve. And with Sandburg there was always a conscientious and sustained commitment to present the problem of class struggle.

This book aims to help readers understand the works of Carl Sandburg and to give them a better sense of Sandburg's contributions to, and influence on, American literature in the twentieth century.

This book specifically explores how Carl Sandburg's life and massive literary output after 1920 not only reveals an important and significant continuity in his political agenda but an important broadening in its breadth and scope as well. Like the works published before 1920, his post-1920 works offer an extremely complex and fascinating political project, one that involves cross-pollinations and complex negotiations of different strands of Socialism, but is more pragmatic than faithful to the party line.

This book also covers several major ideas. First, it attempts to articulate and understand the factors that have contributed to Carl Sandburg's declining trajectory, which has led to a reputation that has diminished significantly in the twentieth century. I note that from the outset of his long career of publication—running from 1904 to 1963—Sandburg was a literary outsider despite (and sometimes because of) his great public popularity though he enjoyed an almost unparalleled national reputation from the early 1920s onward. The book also clarifies how Carl Sandburg, in various ways, was attempting to reinvent or reconstruct American literature. Indeed, beginning in 1920, a very complex creative imagination—one not seen before—begins to manifest itself in his works. As a result, readers begin to see how Sandburg's own view of his role as a writer was shifting—from one of a radical political poet into one of a writer who experimented with different literary genres.

The book also examines the two separately published biographies of Abraham Lincoln—*Abraham Lincoln: The Prairie Years* (1926) and *Abraham Lincoln: The War Years* (1939)—and reveals how Sandburg incorporates a new perspective that was radically different from the Lincoln biographies that preceded it. The book then turns to Sandburg's celebration of the theme of "the People," exploring four works—*The American Songbag* (1927), *Good Morning, America* (1928), *The People, Yes* (1936), and *Remembrance Rock* (1948). Like all of his previous works, these works are an effort to make life possible to the common man. Finally, the book reminds readers of Sandburg's stature as witness to the labor problem—perhaps the most significant problem of the twentieth century. I argue that the only way to recover Sandburg correctly is to assess the political ideology and the use of a new imagination present in each of his published works. In writing this book, I looked at the best published books and articles on Carl Sandburg. The book cites over 140 sources.

—EV
McAllen, Texas

Chronology of Carl Sandburg, 1878–1967

1874 August Sandberg and Clara Anderson marry. Both are Swedish immigrants.

1878 Carl Sandburg born January 6th in Galesburg, Illinois; second child and eldest son of August and Clara Sandberg. Baptized Carl August, called Charles.

1883 Lilian Steichen, future wife of Carl Sandburg, born May 1st in Hancock, Michigan.

1891 Leaves school after eighth grade. Works as newsboy, milk delivery boy, and, in subsequent years, as barbershop shoeshine boy and milkman.

1892 Ends his public education in 8th grade so he can begin working.

1896 Sees Robert Todd Lincoln at 40th anniversary of Lincoln-Douglas debate, Knox College, Galesburg.

1897 Rides boxcar to Missouri, Kansas, Nebraska, Colorado, Iowa, and works on railroad section gang, as farmhand, as dishwasher, and at other odd jobs.

1898 On April 26th, enlists in Illinois Volunteers. Serves as private in Puerto Rico during Spanish-American War. Returns to Galesburg and enrolls as special student at Lombard College in Galesburg.

1899 Appointed to West Point but fails written examination in grammar and arithmetic. Enters Lombard College. Serves in town fire department and as school janitor.

1900 In summer, sells stereographs with Fredrick Dickinson.

1901 Becomes editor-in-chief of *The Lombard Review*. Meets Professor Philip Green Wright, a professor at Lombard College, who encourages Sandburg to write.

1902 Leaves college in spring before graduating; wanders country selling stereographs.

1903 Delivers "The Poet of Democracy"—a lecture championing Walt Whitman.

1904 Writes "Inklings & Idlings" articles in *Galesburg Evening Mail* using pseudonym, "Crimson." First poetry and a few prose pieces published as booklet, *In Reckless Ecstasy*, by Professor Philip Green Wright's Asgard Press.

1905 Becomes assistant editor of *To–Morrow* magazine in Chicago, which publishes some of his poems and pieces.

1906 Becomes lecturer on Walt Whitman and other subjects.

1907 Becomes associate editor and advertising man of The Lyceumite, Chicago. Continues lecturing at Elbert Hubbard's chautauquas. Asgard Press publishes *Incidentals*. Becomes organizer for Social–Democratic Party of Wisconsin. Meets Lilian Steichen, schoolteacher and fellow Socialist.

1908 Publishes *The Plaint of a Rose*. Marries Lilian Steichen on June 15th. Thereafter uses "Carl," not "Charles," as given name. Campaigns in Wisconsin with Socialist presidential candidate Eugene V. Debs. Writes pamphlet "You and Your Job."

1909 Becomes advertising copywriter for Kroeger's Department Store in Milwaukee, then reporter for *Milwaukee Sentinel, Journal*, and *Daily News*.

1910 Father dies March 10th. Becomes private secretary to Emil Seidel, Socialist mayor of Milwaukee. Becomes city editor of *Milwaukee Social-Democratic Herald*. Works for Victor Berger's Conference for Progressive Political Action, a Socialist farm-labor alliance.

1911 Daughter Margaret born June 3rd.

1912 Writes for Berger's *Milwaukee Leader*. Moves to Chicago, briefly joins *Evening World*.

1913 Joins *The Day Book, Chicago*, then *System*, a management magazine, for which he writes under pseudonym R. E. Coulson. Writes under pseudonym Sidney Arnold for *American Artisan & Hardware Record*.

1914 Returns to *The Day Book*, poems published in March issue of *Poetry: A Magazine of Verse*. Wins Helen Haire Levinson Prize for best poems of the year. Moves to Maywood, a Chicago suburb.

1915 Writes articles on "That Walsh Report" and "Fixing the Pay of Railroad Men" for *The International Socialist Review*. Ezra Pound includes Sandburg in his *Catholic Anthology, 1914–1915*, which includes the first appearance of T. S. Eliot's "The Love Song of J. Alfred Prufrock."

1916 Writes four poems for *The Little Review*. *Chicago Poems* published by Henry Holt. Daughter Janet born June 27th. Writes "The Works of Ezra Pound" for *Poetry* magazine, praising Pound's works.

1917 Covers labor conference for the American Federation of Labor at Omaha and Minneapolis Labor Convention. Joins *Chicago Daily News*. Amy Lowell discusses Sandburg, Frost, and other poets in her book, *Tendencies in Modern American Poetry*.

1918 Joins *Chicago Evening* briefly, then Newspaper Enterprise Association. Goes to Stockholm, Sweden. Daughter Helga born November 24th. *Cornhuskers* published by Henry Holt. Returns to New York.

1918 Becomes war correspondent during World War I.

1919 Moves to NEA office in Chicago. Rejoins *Chicago Daily News* as labor reporter; becomes movie reviewer. Shares Poetry Society of America Prize with Margaret Widdemer. Harcourt, Brace and Howe publishes *The Chicago Race Riots*. Moves to Elmhurst, a Chicago suburb. Louis Untermeyer discusses Carl Sandburg in his book, *The New Era in American Poetry*; Conrad Aiken discusses Carl Sandburg in his book, *Skepticisms, Notes on Contemporary Poetry.*

1920 *Smoke and Steel* published by Harcourt, Brace and Howe.

1921 Shares Poetry Society of America Annual Book Award with Stephen Vincent Benét. Champions Walt Whitman in his eight-page Introduction to Harvard College Library's Modern Library edition of *Leaves of Grass*.

1921 Carl Sandburg is already a celebrity of sorts, working schools and colleges, women's lyceums, and chautauqua for a set fee of $125.00.

1922 *Rootabaga Stories* and *Slabs of the Sunburnt West* published by Harcourt, Brace and Company, now Harcourt Brace Jovanovich.

1923 *Rootabaga Pigeons* published.

1926 Two-volume *Abraham Lincoln: The Prairie Years* published by Harcourt, which publishes the rest of his major works. Officially becomes Abraham Lincoln's twentieth-century ambassador and heir. Buys summer cottage at Tower Hill, Michigan. Mother dies December 30. Harriet Monroe discusses Carl Sandburg in her book, *Poets and Their Art*. Carl Sandburg's fame begins to grow.

1927 *The American Songbag* published. Buys land in Harbert, Michigan, on which to build home. Has now performed at over two-thirds of American universities in the country giving his lecture/recital.

1928 Receives Litt. D. from Lombard College. Moves to Harbert. *Good Morning, America, Abe Lincoln Grows Up*, and the first 26 chapters of *Abraham Lincoln: The Prairie Years* are published.

1929 Receives Litt. D. from Knox College. *Steichen the Photographer* and *Rootabaga Country* published.

1930 *Potato Face* and *Early Moon* published.

1931 Receives Litt. D. from Northwestern University. Sister Martha Goldstone dies.

1932 Leaves *Chicago Daily News* in May. *Mary Lincoln: Wife and Widow* published.

1936 *The People, Yes* published.

1938 Receives Order of the North Star from King of Sweden. Appears on the cover of *Life* magazine on February 21st.

1939 Four-volume *Abraham Lincoln: The War Years* published. Appears on the cover of *Time* magazine on December 4th.

1940 Wins Pulitzer Prize in History. Elected to American Academy of Arts and Letters. Receives Litt. D. degrees from Harvard, Yale, Wesleyan and New York Universities, and Lafayette College.

1941 Receives Litt. D. from Syracuse University and Dartmouth College. Grandson John Carl born December 3rd to Helga.

1942 Writes weekly column for *Chicago Times* syndicate, commentary for U.S. Government film *Bomber*, foreign broadcasts for Office of War Information, captions for "Road to Victory" exhibit at Museum of

Modern Art. *Storm Over the Land* published, excerpted from *Abraham Lincoln: The War Years*. Publishes "Those Who Make Poems" in *The Atlantic* in March.

1943 *Home Front Memo* published. Granddaughter Karlen Paula born June 28th to Helga.

1944 *The Photographs of Abraham Lincoln*, with Frederick Hill Meserve, published. Brother Martin Sandburg dies April 7th.

1945 Moves to Connemara Farm, Flat Rock, North Carolina, in late fall. Family pays $40,000 for the 240-acre farm. Records album: *Carl Sandburg: Cowboy Songs and Negro Spirituals*. Is perhaps the most widely known literary figure in the United States.

1946 Birthplace at Galesburg dedicated as historic site.

1948 *Remembrance Rock* published. Goes to Hollywood to help plan it as a film. Receives LL.D. from Augustana College.

1949 *Lincoln Collector: The Story of Oliver R. Barrett's Great Private Collection* published. Records album: *Carl Sandburg: in a recital from his book "The People, Yes."*

1950 Receives Ph.D. from Uppsala University, Sweden. Publishes *Complete Poems*, which wins Pulitzer Prize for poetry. *The New American Songbag* published.

1952 Receives National Institute of Arts and Letters gold medal for history and biography.

1953 Autobiography *Always the Young Strangers* published. Attends Carl Sandburg Day banquet in Chicago on 75th birthday. Receives Poetry Society of America gold medal. Records album *Carl Sandburg Reads*. Records album *Sandburg Reads Sandburg*.

1954 *Abraham Lincoln: The Prairie Years and The War Years*, a condensation of the six volumes in one, published. Ernest Hemingway wins the Nobel Prize for Literature, but says Carl Sandburg, Isak Dinesen, and Bernard Berenson are more deserving. Carl Sandburg High School dedicated in Orland Park, Illinois.

1955 *Prairie-Town Boy*, a child's version of his autobiography, published. Writes Prologue to *Family of Man*, a book of photographs selected by Edward Steichen. Appears on the cover of *Newsweek* on February 14th.

1956 Paid $30,000 by University of Illinois for manuscripts, library, and papers. Receives Humanities Award from Albert Einstein College of Medicine. November 18th proclaimed Carl Sandburg Day in Chicago.

1957 *The Sandburg Range*, an anthology of his work, published. Records *The Great Carl Sandburg*. Records *A Lincoln Album: Readings by Carl Sandburg* (a two-LP set).

1958 Named "Honorary Ambassador" of North Carolina on March 27th, Sandburg Day in Raleigh, North Carolina. Sister Mary Johnson dies July 29th.

1959 Delivers Lincoln Day address February 12th before a joint session of Congress to celebrate Lincoln's 150th birthday. Visits Moscow with Edward Steichen under State Department auspices for "Family of Man" Exhibit. Travels to Stockholm for Swedish-American Day and receives *Litteris et Artibus* medal from King Gustav. Carl Sandburg Junior High School opens in Golden Valley, Minnesota.

1960 Works in Hollywood as consultant for film *The Greatest Story Ever Told*. Publishes volumes *Harvest Poems 1910–1960* and *Wind Song*, poems for children. Norman Corwin's *The World of Carl Sandburg* premieres on Broadway, starring Bette Davis, Clark Allen, and Leif Erickson.

1961 Carl Sandburg visits with John F. Kennedy in the White House on October 5th. Speaks to a group of over 20,000 people on the east front of the United States Capitol to deliver another speech on Lincoln, this one commemorating the 100th anniversary of Lincoln's First Inaugural Address.

1962 Designated poet laureate of Illinois. Writes Foreword to John F. Kennedy's *To Turn the Tide*. Records *The Poetry of Carl Sandburg Read by the Author*

1963 *Honey and Salt* published. Receives International United Poets Award as "Honorary Poet Laureate of the U.S.A."

1964 Receives Presidential Medal of Freedom from Lyndon B. Johnson. Records *Carl Sandburg: Cowboy Songs and Negro Spirituals*.

1967 Dies July 22nd at home in Flat Rock, North Carolina, at age 89. His death is treated as a major news event, appearing on the front page of the *New York Times* and many other newspapers. National Memorial Service held on September 17th at the Lincoln Memorial in Washington D.C. President Lyndon B. Johnson speaks, along with others.

1972 LP released posthumously: *Carl Sandburg: Flat Rock Ballads*. His home in Flat Rock, North Carolina, is officially designated a national historic site, the first writer in the history of our nation to receive this honor; previously, only homes of presidents were designated as such.

1977 Lilian Steichen Sandburg dies February 18th at age 94.

Chapter 1

"Two Men Speak in Mr. Sandburg, a Poet and a Propagandist: His Future Will Depend Upon Which Finally Dominates the Other"

The title of this chapter comes from the opening lines of Amy Lowell's review of Carl Sandburg's third volume of poetry titled *Smoke and Steel* published in 1920. The review was titled "Poetry and Propaganda," and it appeared in the *New York Times* on October 24th of that year. Amy Lowell begins by writing:

> Two men speak in Mr. Sandburg, a poet and a propagandist. His future will depend on which finally dominates the other. Since a poet must speak by means of suggestion and a propagandist succeeds by virtue of clear presentation, in so far as a propagandist is a poet, just in that ratio is he a failure where his propaganda is concerned. On the other hand, the poet who leaves the proper sphere of his art to preach, even by analogy, must examine the mote in his verse very carefully lest, perchance, it turn out a beam. (qtd. in Marowski 340)

She goes on to voice a concern about Sandburg's work when she announces with ominous certainty: "Then [in 1917] I had only one book to go upon [*Chicago Poems*], now I have three, and the danger seems to me to be looming larger with terrific speed" (qtd. in Marowski 340).

With incredible accuracy and impressive foresight, in these statements Amy Lowell—pointing out Carl Sandburg's allegiance to both art and propaganda—foreshadows the dilemma that would plague him during his entire career. Her review also anticipates Carl Sandburg's reputation today—an academic reputation that Brian M. Reed describes in his article "Carl Sandburg's *The People, Yes*, Thirties, Modernism, and Problem of Bad Political Poetry" (2004) as that of an "author of a handful of sincere but clumsy 1910s lyrics best appreciated by readers uneducated in subtleties of form, technique, and tone" (189).

Amy Lowell had pointed out the same danger in Carl Sandburg's practice three years earlier in her book *Tendencies in Modern American Poetry* (1917), a book which explored the "new movement" in American poetry by focusing on the significance and modernity in works by Edwin Arlington Robinson, Robert Frost, Edgar Lee Masters, Carl Sandburg, and two of the leading names in the Imagist movement, H.D. and John Gould Fletcher. Although Amy Lowell includes a lengthy and largely favorable, thirty-two page review of Carl Sandburg's first book of poetry *Chicago Poems* (1916) in her study, already she reveals an awareness of an ever-present political ideology in many of Sandburg's poems. She concludes her assessment of his first book of poetry by registering the following charge:

> Judged from the standard of pure art, it is a pity that so much of Mr. Sandburg's work concerns itself with entirely ephemeral phenomena. The problems of posterity will be other than those which claim our attention. Art, nature, humanity, are eternal. But the minimum wage will probably matter as little to the twenty-second century as it did to the thirteenth, although for different reasons.
>
> Mr. Sandburg has not the broad outlook to achieve the epic quality of Mr. Masters' work. He is a lyric poet, but the lyrist in him has a hard time to make itself heard above the brawling of the market-place.
>
> It is dangerous to give a final verdict on contemporary art. All that one can safely say of Mr. Sandburg's work is that it contains touches of great and original beauty, and whatever posterity may feel about it taken merely as poetry, it cannot fail to hold its place to students of this period as a necessary link in an endless chain. (Lowell 231–32)

In the years since Lowell published her two accounts, the issue regarding Carl Sandburg's relevance, place, and significance as an American writer has slowly been resolving itself. Today, the assessment of Carl Sandburg's poetry and prose—a view that is seemingly definitive—is that he is a minor figure in American literature.

But how and why did Sandburg lose his standing as one of the central literary figures of the twentieth century, especially considering the hundreds of laudatory assessments of his work like that offered by Harry Wolcott Robbins and William Harold Coleman in their 1938 anthology, *Western World Literature*:

> It is the opinion of more than one competent judge that the outstanding figure in American poetry since Whitman is Carl Sandburg, who uses sledge-hammer words to express his deep contempt of those sinister forces in American life that seek to brutalize and dehumanize the souls and bodies of the men and women within their power. (Robbins and Coleman 1299)

Understanding why Carl Sandburg's reputation has diminished significantly since 1938 will be the first of several issues to be explored in this study as it examines the factors that have contributed to the declining trajectory in his reputation. It is important to note that from the outset of his long career of publication—running from 1904 to 1963—Sandburg was a literary outsider despite (and sometimes because of) his great public popularity, though he enjoyed a national reputation from the early 1920s on. For decades after, he carried on running wars with the literary elite, including William Carlos Williams and Robert Frost. Here, it is important to note a second principal reason for his literary diminution: when Carl Sandburg's work first appeared in *Poetry: A Magazine of Verse* in 1913 he was deemed too radical; by the 1920s he was already considered too dated and propagandistic. In essence, because he had written so much so quickly and had experienced great and immediate success, by 1922 Sandburg's reputation as a propagandist was fixed.

As a result, students as well as scholars of American literature have glossed over Sandburg's post-1920 publications, a corpus that constitutes the great majority of his writings. Because of this initial neglect, his work published after 1920 has never been fully explored or analyzed. Even critical assessments offered of his work decades later, including the great majority of the many articles published about his works since 1950, persistently fail to grant Carl Sandburg an adequate reading. Taken together, this misguided collective analysis of his post-1920 works—set in motion by an initial neglect and misreading—coupled with the influence of fashionable literary trends of the twentieth century, has significantly affected Sandburg's standing as a canonical figure. This study will document those shifts and show how a majority of the leading critical assessments of his work published after 1920 have completely overlooked the distinct possibility that the political ideology in Carl Sandburg's poetry and prose—one that is ever-present and extremely cohesive—should be seen as a strength rather than a weakness.

A close study of his publications after 1920 will also reveal a literary man with a fertile and creative mind whose works present an evolving, yet coherent, political ideology that is deeply rooted in the tenets of the Socialist Party of America, the Industrial Workers of the World (IWW), and the American Federation of Labor (AFL). Brian Reed incisively notes "With only one prominent exception   Sally Greene's '"Things Money Cannot Buy": Carl Sandburg's Tribute to Virginia Woolf'—critics have not inquired at length into Sandburg's post-1920 writings or politics" (186). A study of this political ideology present throughout his massive literary corpus has never been adequately pursued. Doing so will reveal, as Cary Nelson has stated, that Sandburg's work has not only been misread, but serves to persuade audiences to be "reoccupied with a newly politicized self-awareness" (Nelson 915).

Although his poetry and prose do not so much encompass as expand a point of view, a close examination of Carl Sandburg's writings after 1920 will reveal an extremely conscientious and careful writer who, contrary to most critical assessments, held and maintained a consistent theory for writing as well as a coherent worldview. His sense of writerly vocation reveals much about him, including a persistent sense of time and place. For example, his earliest works present a "disillusionment with post-World War I America which anticipates T. S. Eliot's" (Ferguson, Salter, and Stallworthy 1167). Sandburg was, indeed, actively participating in many of the literary trends that typify Modern literature as well as the Modernist Poetry movement, but assessments of Sandburg—even early ones—overlook his participation in the literary preoccupations of the time.

For the New Critics, Sandburg's poetry held few interesting ambiguities, intentional or unintentional. There were no puzzles, no obscure allusions, and no varied levels of meaning. Elitism also worked against his reputation. Many critics were unwilling to find either literary or intellectual grace in a man whose books were read by millions, who always headed the best seller lists, and who lived a financially comfortable life. In 1972, Gay Wilson Allen said that Sandburg suffered from the "curse of success" (Allen, "Carl Sandburg" 2). Such a poet must not be very good, it was thought. He must be writing to the lowest level of the public's comprehension on subjects that are pedestrian or insignificant.

Nonetheless, Carl Sandburg can still be read with profit. As Cary Nelson has illustrated in his essay "The Diversity of American Poetry," which appears in the *Columbia Literary History of the United States* (1988), Sandburg was writing at a time when the nature and function of modern poetry, and by extension the role of the literary critic, were still greatly contested (Nelson 913). Much of the literature of the early- to mid-twentieth century did indeed explore the relationship between labor and capitalism, and it centers on exploring the misery in the lives of the "working class," a term used with great frequency by labor organizations, intellectuals, and writers. This literature is one of social analysis and protest, a "fiction [in the broadest sense] that takes the businessman or economic condition as its focus" (Brooks, Lewis, and Warren 780), and the output on the subject by a wide range of authors is impressive. Many writers, like Carl Sandburg, who early on saw himself principally as a chronicler of labor issues, offered consistent and compelling indictments of corporate greed as well as heedless urban growth and exposed the problems facing the American working class.

Carl Sandburg certainly felt that he was writing about timely issues. As a man of letters, he was, indeed, one of the most celebrated "political" voices. His post-1920 works were being read by millions of Americans, and what he had to say was seen as significant. During his entire literary career, Carl Sandburg saw himself as a literary figure who wanted to bring poetry and prose to the masses, and he did that with great success. But as Brian Reed points out in "Carl Sandburg's *The People, Yes*, Thirties Modernism, and the Problem of Bad Political Poetry" (2004), beginning in the 1940s and continuing into the 1950s, "academic consensus on what constitutes poetic merit represent[ed] the victory of an ostensibly apolitical formalism. … The diverse, vibrant radical poetries of the 1930s disappeared almost completely from view" (Reed 183). After this period, it became received academic wisdom that technique, diction, tone, and other formal aspects of a poem are crucial to its value, whereas overt political and ethical commitments were said to be of secondary importance. As a result, since 1950 most assessments of Sandburg have been negative. It is hardly surprising that he has been almost permanently displaced from his standing as a canonical figure in the literature of this country.

A majority of critical assessments, including recent ones, fail because they do not capture the complexity of his "technique, diction, tone, and the other formal aspects of a poem crucial to its value," (Reed 183) nor do these assessments capture his political ideology. While it is true that Carl Sandburg broke with the Socialist Party in 1916 and never again subscribed to any specific political agenda, the undergirding for his newly formed politics remained firmly fixed in Socialist ideology and clearly echo positions articulated by the three leading labor organizations in America during the early years of the twentieth century. As with the leaders of the IWW, for Sandburg "abstract doctrine meant nothing to the disinherited; specific grievances meant everything" (Dubofsky 90). To correct the record, it must be made clear that the vast majority of Sandburg's post-1920 poetry and prose does not consist of "abstract doctrine" as many scholars of American Literature believe; instead, it deals with the concrete problems created by urban industrial life.

Chapter 2

Carl Sandburg's Early Works and Themes, and Critical
Assessments of His Early Works (1916–1930)

C arl Sandburg's literary career began in 1904 with an independently pub-
lished slim volume of poems and essays titled *In Reckless Ecstasy*. Three
additional independently published short prose works, *Incidentals* (1907), *The
Plaint of a Rose* (1908), and *Joseffy* (1910) soon followed. Although Sandburg
was still honing his craft during these early years, he was already working with
many of the central themes he would continue to develop during his extremely
long literary career that stretched from 1904 to 1967. The earliest and most
central theme that appears in *In Reckless Ecstasy* is a strong, deep interest and
respect for the common laboring man, as seen in the poem "To Whom My Hand
Goes Out":

> The unapplauded ones who bear
> No badges on their breasts,
> Who pass us on the street, with calm,
> Unfearing, patient eyes,
> Like dumb car-horses in the sleet!
> The unperturbed who feel the oldness—
> All the sadness of the world—
> Yet somehow feel the sacredness
> Of grime upon their hands,
> And even know the rush of pity
> For the ones who know not
> That some Power builds a callus out of blisters.
> The eyes! The eyes that pierce
> The dust and smoke of unrewarded toil
> And count it gain and joy
> To have lived and sweat and wrought
> And been a man! (Sandburg, *In Reckless Ecstasy* 18)

This interest in the common laboring man would persist in all of Carl Sandburg's works published thereafter. Beginning with *Chicago Poems* (1916), his later works begin to incorporate very specific ideological tenets that belong to the Socialist Labor Party of America, the American Federation of Labor (AFL), and the Industrial Workers of the World (IWW), whose headquarters were located, coincidentally, in Sandburg's Chicago. Virtually every volume of poetry and prose, including what is now his most celebrated book of poetry, *The People, Yes* (1936), serves as a tribute to the common laboring man in America, but it should be noted that his first volume of poetry and essays also reveals an interest in Abraham Lincoln, as seen in a brief mention in the short selection titled "Wayside Words with Comrades." Beginning with his 1904 publication, Sandburg's *In Reckless Ecstasy* already shows a commitment to exploring the problems inherent in the rise of American industrialism. Not only does Sandburg specifically expose the hardships the common laborer endures daily, but he also underscores the problem of child labor. His short essay titled "Millville"—an actual city in southern New Jersey that Sandburg visited in his early travels around America—describes how children as young as eight and nine work endlessly during the day and on into the night. Sandburg poignantly explains how "Their education has consisted mainly of the thoughts, emotions and experiences that resulted from contact with 'blowers' and 'gaffers,' besides views of a big, barn-like space lit up by white-hot sand" (Sandburg, *In Reckless Ecstasy*, 26). From its earliest stages, Carl Sandburg's prose and poetry shows an interest in Socialism and its tenets; eventually, this concern would grow in scope, breadth, and complexity, and it would manifest itself with tremendous and concentrated force in *Chicago Poems* and, in some way or another, in most of the poetry and prose published thereafter.

Even though Carl Sandburg began his literary career in 1904 with the publication of *In Reckless Ecstasy*, his national literary debut did not occur until March of 1913, when nine of his poems were included in Harriet Monroe's *Poetry: A Magazine of Verse*, a Chicago-based publication that had been founded the year before (Niven 243). Although many critics, including Ezra Pound, immediately saw the potential for genius in Sandburg, the conversations surrounding his central or marginal place in literature also began at that time. In the months following the publication of Sandburg's poems, his reputation was quickly widening and so were the debates in poetry circles concerning whether his work was legitimately poetic (Niven 243).

Considering that the story Carl Sandburg wanted to tell in *Chicago Poems* was a story that was very common at this time in the history of American labor—poverty in the midst of plenty—it is no accident that Carl Sandburg's first professionally published volume of poetry appeared in 1916, following one of the worst three-year industrial depressions and recessions in American history (Dubofsky 9–10). In a letter Sandburg wrote to Amy Lowell on June 10, 1917, he explained:

> I admit there is some animus of violence in *Chicago Poems* but the aim was rather the presentation of motives and character than the furtherance of IWW theories. Of course, I honestly prefer the theories of the IWW to those of the opponents and some of my honest preferences may have crept into the book, as you suggest, but the aim was to sing, blab, chortle, yodel, like people, and people in the sense of human beings subtracted from formal doctrines. (qtd. in Mitgang 117–8)

That Sandburg had a theory for his writing in 1916 is clear. That he had a complex political ideology in 1916 is also clear, and the power and force of this volume of "tradition-shattering" (qtd. in Salwak 2) poetry immediately instigated a plethora of mixed critical assessments. In many ways, this powerful and curious volume of poetry, which received a great deal of interest from his contemporaries, set in motion the trajectory Sandburg's later career would take.

Many of the unfavorable reviews of *Chicago Poems* echoed the concern articulated by Ezra Pound in 1913—that Sandburg's poetry contained awkward phrasings and lacked "form" (Niven 267). William Stanley Braithwaite of the *Boston Transcript* thought that Sandburg's first book of poems was a "book of ill-regulated speech that has neither verse or prose rhythms" (Niven 276). The anonymous reviewer in the *New York Times* described the unevenness in Sandburg's work and asserted that while Sandburg's best is very good, his worst is "dull and shapeless" (qtd. in Salwak 2). It is interesting to note, though, that even with all of the mixed criticism that Carl Sandburg received, the Socialist Party of America believed that *Chicago Poems* helped advance its cause. As a result, many of Sandburg's poems were reprinted repeatedly in Socialist publications throughout the country, including *The International Socialist Review* and *The Masses*, two of the leading Socialist publications in the United States. Of course, it is important to remember that Sandburg had been an extremely active member of the Socialist Party since 1907, but left the party in 1916 (Niven 285).

Charges of Sandburg's stylistic shortcomings and deficiencies were not only raised after the publication of *Chicago Poems* but also remained consistent throughout his career. For example, in July of 1919, three years after the publication of *Chicago Poems*, and after Sandburg was beginning to secure a place for himself as a political writer, William Carlos Williams accused him of producing "ataxic drivel" (Niven 608). The charge was repeated in 1951 in an exhaustively lengthy and now famous review Williams wrote of the *Complete Poems*, in which he charged that Sandburg's poems revealed no technical characteristics "other than their formlessness" and argued that "no motivating spirit ... [controlled them]" (Niven 608). As a high modernist, in both reviews Williams examined Sandburg's works looking for the characteristics that he had been articulating in his essays for many years. As is the case with other critics of Sandburg, Williams was not looking at Sandburg's political project; instead, he demanded to see more of the characteristics of high modernism. Williams wrote to Harriet Monroe in 1913:

> Most current verse is dead from the point of view of art. ... Now life is above all things else at any moment subversive of life as it was the moment before—always new, irregular. Verse to be alive must have infused into it something of the same order, some tincture of disestablishment, something in the nature of impalpable revolution, an ethereal reversal, let me say. I am speaking of modern verse. (qtd. in Ellman and O'Clair 168)

William Carlos Williams, a harsh critic of most of his contemporaries, believed that Carl Sandburg's poetry was "dead from the point of view of art." Additionally, Sandburg's poetry—a poetry that was steeped in political ideology and observations of common life—arrived at a time when the "New Poetry" began eclipsing the political poetry and prose that had been very popular in the late nineteenth and early twentieth centuries. Indeed, Sandburg's *Chicago Poems* do not have "some tincture of disestablishment, something in the nature of *impalpable* revolution, and *ethereal* reversal" (emphases mine). A poem like "And They Obey" reveals the shortcomings Williams found in Sandburg. Sandburg writes:

> Smash down the cities.
> Knock the walls to pieces.
>
> Break down the factories and cathedrals, warehouses and homes Into loose piles of stone and lumber and black burnt wood:
>
> You are soldiers and we command you.
> Build up the cities.
> Set up the walls again.
>
> Put together once more the factories and cathedrals, warehouses and homes Into buildings for life and labor:

You are workmen and citizens all. We command you.
(*Complete Poems* 40)

Sandburg's revolution was conceived in literal, materialistic terms.

Dale Salwak points out in his Introduction to *Carl Sandburg: A Reference Guide* (1988) that Carl Sandburg's work has always been either applauded or dismissed; there is seldom mixed judgment (Salwak xi). In tracing over one thousand annotated bibliographic entries of secondary sources covering Sandburg's career from 1904 to 1987, Salwak demonstrates the shifting trajectory of Sandburg's literary reputation. Interestingly, most poets, as well as the literary and cultural critics who negatively critiqued Sandburg's poetry during his lifetime, based their pronouncements predominantly on his perceived lack of form—Sandburg, of course, was an advocate of free verse. But his politically charged poetry, his political subtext, and his interest in using what seems to be pedestrian language, never captured the interest of the modernists, high modernists, and New Critics. Like Williams, those groups established a set of precepts that would govern the design and structure of twentieth century American poetry. As a result, Carl Sandburg's earliest works were never really seriously examined.

Carl Sandburg's prose received even less critical attention than his poetry. A careful review of his literary reputation finds that the prose he produced, namely the two separate two- and four-volume biographies of Lincoln—the first published in 1926, the second in 1939—as well as the novel published in 1948 and his autobiographical novel published in 1953, were received with a great deal of indifference by those in the Academy as well as by a significant number of his contemporaries. This was a result of the early impressions—that he was not a careful poet and that he published his work with little or no revision.

A close look at the representative critical assessments offered on Sandburg's works reveals a declining trajectory in Carl Sandburg's reputation that began almost immediately at the outset of his career. The first significant wave of critical contempt came in the years between 1916—the year *Chicago Poems* was published—and 1922—the year *Slabs of the Sunburnt West* was published. Not surprisingly, after 1922 he began writing prose almost exclusively and published only three subsequent volumes of poetry: *Good Morning, America* (1928), *The People, Yes* (1936), and a slim volume titled *Honey and Salt* (1963).

As we have seen, Carl Sandburg's poetry published between 1916 and 1922 was produced against a backdrop of regnant Modernism. The American public had been introduced to modern art at the famous New York Armory

Show in 1913, which featured cubist paintings, including Marcel Duchamp's *Nude Descending a Staircase*. At the heart of the modernist aesthetic lay the conviction that

> previously sustaining structures of human life, whether social, political, religious, or artistic, had been either destroyed or shown up as falsehoods or fantasies. To the extent that art incorporated such a false order, it had to be renovated. Order, sequence, and unity in works of art might well be considered only expressions of a desire for coherence rather than actual reflections of reality. ... Thus the defining formal characteristic of the modernist work, whether a painting, a sculpture, or a musical composition, is its construction out of fragments. The long work is an assemblage of fragments, the short work a carefully realized fragment. (Baym 944)

Important poetry published between 1916 and 1922 included works by Ezra Pound, Amy Lowell, H.D., Edwin Arlington Robinson, Wallace Stevens, William Carlos Williams, Edgar Lee Masters, Marianne Moore, John Crowe Ransom, Hart Crane, T. S. Eliot, and Robert Frost. These modernist works "assumed a disjunction between art and life: meaning not revealed but made. Construction was itself the cognitive act: mastery of the medium disclosed the form of perception, organic now not to the operations of nature but to the internal relations of its structure" (Preminger and Brogan 55). But, as Williams and other critics pointed out, Sandburg's poetry revealed that he was not entirely participating in this movement.

In 1912, Ezra Pound and H.D. launched the Imagist Movement in poetry, "demanding direct treatment of the thing," regardless of whether the thing was inside or outside the mind. A few years later Pound shifted his attention from Imagism to Vorticism, emphasizing the dynamism of content. Carl Sandburg was writing within this dynamic and experimental literary Zeitgeist. And though overtly political literature was still being published, it was slowly being eclipsed by the "New Poetry." Amy Lowell's book mentioned earlier, *Tendencies in Modern American Poetry*, reveals the trends in poetry that Carl Sandburg was up against, specifically as represented by Edwin Arlington Robinson, Robert Frost, Edgar Lee Masters, H.D., and John Gould Fletcher. For all of these poets, injecting a political subtext and promoting a political ideology was seldom a concern; instead, these poets were experimenting entirely with subject matter and style. In many ways, between 1916 and 1922 Carl Sandburg was daring to write a type of poetry that had been losing critical esteem since 1900.

This may very well have been one of the reasons he turned his back on poetry in 1922. A review of the critical response to *Chicago Poems* shows that out of the fourteen published notices, including favorable reviews written by notable literary figures such as Amy Lowell, Harriet Monroe, and Louis Untermeyer, a total of eight offer laudatory assessments while the remaining six emphasize Sandburg's "lack of skill" (qtd. in Salwak 3) and complain of a "technique and substance [that often] angers [readers] (qtd. in Salwak 2). However, it is important to note that even a laudatory assessment like the one offered by William Aspenwall Bradley in the December issue of *The Dial* raises the following concern: "There are two Sandburgs: the clever reporter (rather gross, simpleminded, sentimental, sensual man among men) and the true artist (highly sensitized impressionist) belonging with the Imagists" (qtd. in Salwak 2). (Bradley's observation coincidentally echoes the concern raised by Amy Lowell in her 1917 book *Tendencies in Modern American Poetry*). Ultimately, this first view of Sandburg won out—Sandburg was classified prematurely as "the clever reporter (rather gross, simpleminded, sentimental, sensual man among men)," and almost any poem in *Chicago Poems* supports this. For example, the poem "Anna Imroth" reads as follows:

> Cross the hands over the breast here—so.
> Straighten the legs a little more—so.
> And call for the wagon to come and take her home.
> Her mother will cry some and so will her sisters and brothers.
>
> But all of the others got down and they are safe and this is the only
> one of the factory girls who wasn't lucky in making the jump when
> the fire broke.
> It is the hand of God and lack of fire escapes.
> (*Complete Poems* 16)

Sandburg, "the clever reporter" writes this poem and, ultimately, the poem seems to advocate a more sensible policy in building codes. In keeping with the charge Williams made, Sandburg's language is pedestrian and "the verse is dead from the point of view of art." But this is Sandburg's style, and this seeming simplicity is what made him and his books popular with the masses.

In 1918, Sandburg published his second volume of poetry, *Cornhuskers*. It shared the second annual Poetry Society of America Prize for the best book of poetry published in the nation with Margaret Widdemer's *The Old Road to Paradise*. Since the Pulitzer Prizes did not yet take poetry into account, the Poetry Society award was particularly prestigious. Nonetheless, the reviews offered of his work in 1918 and 1919 paralleled the reviews of *Chicago Poems*. During this two-year period, ten articles praised Sandburg's poetry and six articles condemned it, including an extremely damning review written by Conrad Aiken in which he concludes that "The sociologist gets in the way of the poet. Like Frost, Masters, Gibson, and Masefield, he searches for 'color and pathos in the lives of the commonplace' but is less selective. Sandburg writes the way he does because he simply cannot do better" (qtd. in Salwak 6).

Published in 1920, *Smoke and Steel* received a similar mixed assessment. This time, over twenty reviews appeared. Half of them were positive, including Louis Untermeyer's article—one of many laudatory reviews he would write over the next thirty years—which appeared in *The New Republic* on December 15, 1920. Untermeyer's assessment is mostly positive, but he, too, expresses a concern:

> He [Sandburg] is a reporter turned mystic. His mood, accent, and image are held at a glowing pitch, fused in a new intensity. But there is a danger here: his thought directs him, so that he becomes the instrument rather than the artist. In spite of this, the book is an epic of modern industrialism and a mighty paean to modern beauty. (qtd. in Salwak 10)

Edmund Wilson's article, "The Anarchists of Taste—Who First Broke the Rules of Harmony with the Modern World" (one of many published over a fifty-year period blasting Sandburg), published in *Vanity Fair* in November of 1920, adds to Untermeyer's assessment of Sandburg. Wilson explains how:

> ... [There is] no ecstasy of beauty here, no calm and high reflection. ... There is nothing in Chicago to encourage a sensitive lover of life. Free verse is the proper vehicle of expression for one coming from the cramped, untrained, and starving poetic feeling of our time. Free verse is appropriate for his half-journalistic impressions of the modern world. When he tries to write a bona fide lyric poem, however, the form is less than adequate. (qtd in Salwak 10)

Sandburg's 1922 volume *Slabs of the Sunburnt West* enjoyed the same high level of interest as his previous volumes, but for the first time in Sandburg's career the negative criticisms against him win out. Malcolm Cowley and William Rose Benét provided two of the three positive reviews, but ten reviews evaluated Sandburg unfavorably. T. S. Eliot explained in the May issue of the *Dial* that "Some of Sandburg's smaller verse is charming; but it appears to be rather an echo of Mr. Pound, who has done it better" (qtd. in Salwak 13).

Although Carl Sandburg did not publish his fifth volume of poetry until 1928 and his sixth until 1936, he continued publishing prose voluminously. In 1922 and 1923, he brought out *Rootabaga Stories* and *Rootabaga Pigeons*—two collections of children's stories. But, even these works were reviewed contemptuously. Mabel H. B. Mussey reviewed *Rootabaga Stories* in the *Nation's* December 6, 1922, issue and implied that no intelligent child could make sense of the collection. A second review in the December 1923 issue of the *Freeman* explains how *Rootabaga Pigeons* is a work that "adults may find charming, but a child of ten will lay the book down with a solemn headshake of bored dissatisfaction" (qtd in Salwak 16). One of the most interesting reviews of *Rootabaga Pigeons* was written by Muna Lee in the *Double Dealer* and argued that Sandburg's fairy tales have "strictly proletarian fairies" (qtd in Salwak 16)—again, another indication of Sandburg's commitment to the idea of celebrating the common man. But more importantly, this statement by Lee helps support the claim that by 1922 Sandburg's reputation had been calcified as that of a radical political ideologue. With the publication of *Rootabaga Stories* and *Rootabaga Pigeons*, though, Carl Sandburg achieved national celebrity status, mostly with children and their parents. This popularity helped to complicate the way his contemporaries saw Sandburg and his work.

When *Abraham Lincoln: The Prairie Years* was published in 1926, close to fifty critical assessments appeared in American magazines and journals. Articles and reviews were written by notable figures including Conrad Aiken, H. L. Mencken, Harriet Monroe, Louis Untermeyer, and Mark Van Doren. Even though reviews of his biography were mixed, Sandburg seemed to gain a second wind as a writer and literary figure, and by this time he had already become, as Louis Untermeyer had stated, the "laureate of industrial America" (qtd in Salwak 26).

For the next few decades, Carl Sandburg continued publishing prolifically, and the mixed critical assessments continued. In 1927 Howard Mumford Jones wrote in the *Virginia Quarterly Review* that Carl Sandburg was "the most richly endowed of all our living poets, and the most unpredictable" (qtd in Salwak 29), but that same year William Carlos Williams, predictably, evaluated Carl Sandburg as "a writer of excellent hokkus" (qtd. in Salwak 35).

Chapter 3

Critical Assessments of His Later Works
(1930–Present)

The number of negative assessments of Sandburg's works grew significantly in the years after 1930, and it is important to note that a significant number of the books written by those in the Academy—books treating American literature as a whole, and anthologies—also presented unfavorable reviews of Sandburg. For example, Fred Lewis Pattee's *The New American Literature* (1890–1930) (1930) argued that Sandburg's writing showed too much sociology and too little artistry. Ludwig Lewisohn's *Expressions in America* (1932), as well as his subsequent book *Story of American Literature* (1937), offered negative assessments of Sandburg's work, while Morton Zabel's *Literary Opinion in America: Essays Illustrating the Status, Methods, and Problems of Criticism in the United States* (1937) argued that Sandburg would be a greater poet if he "worked harder at his social and moral philosophy" (qtd. in Salwak 48). In their book *Outline History of American Literature* (1945), B. V. Crawford, A. C. Kern, and M. H. Needleman argued that Sandburg was a poet of secondary importance. M. L. Rosenfeld's *The Modern Poets* (1960) explained how Sandburg was a minimal stylist who wrote "half poetry." Roy Harvey Pearce's *The Continuity of American Poetry* (1961) points out several of Sandburg's shortcomings, explaining how Sandburg "registered the people's sentiments and did little to enhance or change them" (271). Edmund Wilson's *Patriotic Gore: Studies in the Literature of the American War* (1962), once again, offered a scathing critique of Sandburg and his Lincoln biography.

At the same time as his reputation was being attacked, a number of Sandburg's contemporaries, including some in the Academy, defended him against the consistent charges being leveled both at him and his work. For example, Russell Blankenship's *American Literature as an Expression of the National Mind* (1931) predicted that Sandburg might be credited with initiating a "new and individual poetic form" (qtd. in Salwak 38). Percy H. Boynton's *Literature and American Life for Students of American Literature* (1936) defended the quality of his verse.

Louis Untermeyer's *Modern American Poetry: A Critical Anthology* (1936) offered a completely favorable review of the corpus of his poetry. Cleanth Brooks's *Modern Poetry and the Tradition* (1939) compared Carl Sandburg to Walt Whitman. In *American and British Literature Since 1890* (1939), Carl and Mark Van Doren—both long-time active advocates of Sandburg's work—demonstrated an excited enthusiasm for Sandburg's poetry. Fred Millett's *Contemporary American Authors* (1941) evaluated him as a better poet than Vachel Lindsay and Edgar Lee Masters. Henry W. Wells's *The American Way of Poetry* (1943) positioned him as a central figure in the field of American literature. Mixed responses to Sandburg's reputation persisted through 1950.

Although Carl Sandburg received the Pulitzer Prize for Poetry in 1951 for his *Complete Poems* (1950), his reputation in its totality, at least as seen by those in the Academy, was significantly fading. This fading reputation was punctuated with what has now become the most famous review offered of Sandburg's *Complete Poems*, written by William Carlos Williams—a review Carl Sandburg ironically asked Williams to write. In many ways, this review, which appeared in *Poetry* in September of 1951, remains the most damning review ever offered of Sandburg's poetry, and in many ways it represents the beginning of the end of his career. Many of the charges registered by Williams serve as a composite of the negative assessments that had been leveled against Sandburg by his critics.

William Carlos Williams's review of *Complete Poems* was one Carl Sandburg "never forgave." In it, Williams registers the following charges:

> Search as we will among them we must say at once that technically the poems reveal no initiative whatever other than their formlessness; there is no motivating spirit held in the front of the mind to control them. And without a theory, as Pasteur once said, to unite it, a man's life becomes little more than an aimless series of random and repetitious gestures. In the poem a rebellion against older forms means nothing unless, finally, we have a new form to substitute for that which has become empty from the exhaustion of its means. There never has been any positive value in the form or lack of form known as free verse into which Sandburg's verse is cast. (Williams, *Selected Essays* 272)

Later in the review Williams writes:

> When Picasso became a Communist, convinced that was his human duty, it did NOT alter his dedication to his task as an artist. And the official Communist Blackguards were forced to accept his point of view, not he theirs. They did NOT suppress him.

> But Sandburg, convinced that the official democracy he was witness-
> ing was rotten, abandoned his art to expose it. He suffered the inevitable
> results. He knew what he was doing. To have persisted as a pure poet
> would have maimed what to him was the outstanding thing: the report of
> the people, the basis of all art and of everything that is alive with regenera-
> tive power.
>
> He didn't see that the terms the people use are so often the very
> thing that defeats them. It is by his invention of new terms that the artist
> uniquely serves. The process is much more complex than Sandburg real-
> izes. (276)

Finally, Williams says:

> In this massive book [*Complete Poems*] covering a period of close to forty
> years the poems show no development of the thought, in the technical
> handling of the material, in the knowledge of the forms, the art of treating
> the line. The same manner of using the words, of presenting the image is
> followed in the first poem as in the last. All that can be said is that a horde
> walks steadily, unhurriedly through its pages, following without affection
> one behind the other. (277)

Coincidentally, William Carlos Williams's review of Sandburg's *Complete Poems* was published only six months after Gay Wilson Allen—a long-time advocate of Sandburg—reviewed the same Pulitzer Prize-winning book, argu-ing that Sandburg was a positivist who let facts speak for themselves. Allen added, contrary to Williams, that Sandburg had learned to be a better writer through the passing years, having outgrown his myth of the virile and provincial Midwesterner. Already in his seventies when he received his second Pulitzer Prize—the first had been given to him in 1940 for his work on *Abraham Lincoln: The War Years*—Carl Sandburg did not publish anything significant after 1950. All of his best work had been written.

What followed after 1950 was a continuation and, in many ways, a resolution of the debate regarding Carl Sandburg's place in American literature, a debate that had been taking place since 1913. Part of what complicates this debate has to do with Sandburg's publication history. After all, a majority of his publications after 1922 were works of prose, with the bulk of his publication be-ing represented by two separate biographies on Abraham Lincoln. Additionally, Carl Sandburg published eight children's books, which include *Rootabaga Stories* (1922), *Rootabaga Pigeons* (1923), *Abe Lincoln Grows Up* (1928), *Potato Face* (1930), *Early Moon* (1930), *Prairie-Town Boy* (1955), *Wind Song, and The*

Wedding Procession of the Rag Doll and the Broom Handle Who Was in It (1967). As noted earlier, very little poetry was published after 1922. After 1950 criticisms of Sandburg became more unforgiving. For example, the anonymous review of Carl Sandburg's *Always the Young Strangers* (1953), published on January 12, 1953, in *Time* magazine, notes "an artless lack of point and discrimination that flirts perilously with final boredom" (qtd. in Salwak). On the same day, though, the anonymous review in *Newsweek* described Carl Sandburg's story as "almost perfect background for expressions of esteem from his fellow men" (qtd. in Salwak).

Carl Sandburg's curse and, at the same time, his saving grace is that he published voluminously—more than thirty-five books. Included are—surprisingly—only six volumes of poetry, several miscellaneous pieces of nonfiction, including *The Chicago Race Riots, July 1919* (1919) and *Steichen the Photographer* (1929), as well as works of fiction and three biographies—two of Abraham Lincoln and a separate volume on Mary Todd Lincoln titled *Mary Lincoln: Wife and Widow* (1932). In addition, Carl Sandburg published an autobiography, a book of songs, eight children's stories, along with hundreds of contributions to periodicals and anthologies, Forewords, Introductions, and foreign editions. As a matter of fact, between 1916 and 1967 Carl Sandburg had at least one new publication on the shelves of American bookstores every two or three years. He was such a prominent cultural figure in America that he appeared on the cover of *Life* magazine in 1938 and on the cover of *Time* magazine in 1939. This pattern—public acclamation, on the one hand, and critical dismissiveness, on the other—would repeat itself again and again.

However, in the years after 1950, in many ways the dust began to settle concerning Carl Sandburg's place in the landscape of American Literature. Since then, critical commentary about Sandburg has been limited, but what does appear seems to still wrestle with the issue posed by Amy Lowell at the outset of this study. For example, in a recently published article (2004), Brian Reed argues that

> Sandburg's popular appeal has not translated into enduring academic respect. The last twenty years have seen a surprising paucity of work on his writing. There has been one comprehensive biography—Penelope Niven's *Carl Sandburg* (1991)—one substantial book-length study—Philip Yannella's *The Other Carl Sandburg* (1996)—a recent study of Sandburg's literary milieu—Lisa Woolley's *American Voices of the Chicago Renaissance* (2000)—and a handful of articles. This meager showing cannot begin to compare to the literary-critical industries that have grown up

around such other American modernists as Hart Crane, H.D., T. S. Eliot,
Ezra Pound, and William Carlos Williams. (185)

Indeed, the little that has appeared about Sandburg in recent decades, plus
the fact that he had already become a marginal figure in the field of American
Literature since about 1951, serves as irrefutable evidence that his reputation as
a mere "propagandist" and as a writer of "clumsy verses" has won out. Tragically,
American literary study seems to have little interest in Sandburg or in much of
the propagandist art produced by a plethora of American writers. A close look
at almost any of the standard literature anthologies used in college classrooms
today easily supports this point.

For example, the list of literary works written and published in the late
nineteenth and early twentieth centuries that focus on issues like corporate
greed, heedless urban growth, and the problems facing the "working class" is
seemingly endless. A preliminary list of significant pieces would include some
of the following: Frank Norris's *McTeague* (1899), *The Octopus* (1901), and *The
Pit* (1903); William Dean Howells's *The Rise of Silas Lapham* (1885) and *A
Hazard of New Fortunes* (1890); Edward Bellamy's *Looking Backward* (1888);
Stephen Crane's *Maggie: A Girl of the Streets* (1893); Upton Sinclair's *The Jungle*
(1906); Jack London's *The Iron Heel* (1907); Theodore Dreiser's *The Financier*
(1912) and *The Titan* (1914); David Graham Phillips's *Susan Lenox: Her Fall
and Rise* (1917); and Carl Sandburg's *Chicago Poems* (1916), *Cornhuskers* (1918),
and *Smoke and Steel* (1920). Significant literary works published after 1920 that
"take the businessman or economic conditions" as their focus include Sinclair
Lewis's *Babbitt* (1922), Clifford Odets's plays, including *Waiting for Lefty* (1935);
Michael Gold's anthology *Proletarian Literature in the United States* (1935); and
John Steinbeck's *The Grapes of Wrath* (1939).

One point that must be underscored before continuing is that this literature
that took labor and the "working class" as its central issue ran parallel to and
kept pace with the evolving labor issues in the country. In other words, literary
works of mass social movements and social protest made an effort to capture
the essence of what was a consistently changing political landscape and con-
versation. To put it even more simply, works of mass social movements written
in the early part of the twentieth century treat specific issues of labor that are
unique to that period of time and differ widely in scope from works published a
decade or two later. Within the genre of the literature of mass social movements
is great diversity and evolution, and the literature of many socially conscious
twentieth-century writers reveals this shift. Part of the reason for this diversity

and evolution can be traced to ongoing intellectual conversations concerning labor and the creation of a "working class," as well as the many labor organizations articulating political ideologies that attracted millions of individuals belonging to this new "working class."

It is central to point out that the history of the labor problem in America at the turn of the century is still an important issue that is carefully covered in a majority of college-level American history textbooks today. And the relevant literature produced during the last decade of the nineteenth century and the first half of the twentieth century is still discussed at length in many American history courses. Surprisingly, though, for several decades now, literature anthologies have not devoted significant attention to this period of American history or to any of the literary works mentioned above—works that serve as compelling indictments of corporate greed and heedless urban growth affecting the working class. For example, Frank Norris's labor novels are ignored in most American literature courses. The *Norton* editors only include his essay "A Plea for Romantic Fiction" (1901). The only two works included by William Dean Howells are "Novel-Writing and Novel-Reading" (1899) and "Editha" (1907). Edward Bellamy is overlooked altogether, and the only works included by Stephen Crane are his famous short stories, "The Open Boat," "The Bride Comes to Yellow Sky," "The Blue Hotel," and "An Episode of War." The only two works included by Jack London are "The Law of Life" and "To Build a Fire." Nothing by Upton Sinclair is included, and the only work included by Theodore Dreiser is "Old Ragaum and His Theresa."

At many levels, this literary sampling is not only a misrepresentation of these writers, but it is also a misrepresentation of this period in American history and American literature.

Likewise, and not surprisingly, Carl Sandburg has been misrepresented as a literary figure since the mid-twentieth century. Daniel Hoffman's "Sandburg and 'The People': His Literary Populism Reappraised," published in June of 1950 in the *Antioch Review*, accurately explains how Sandburg has lost modern poetry's serious readers because he has presented collective emotions divorced from the individual consciousness. Hoffman adds that Sandburg's style has alienated those who see Eliot, Pound, and Wallace Stevens as chief poetic spokesmen. Like William Carlos Williams, Hoffman makes the point that Sandburg only registers the sentiments of the people and does nothing to enhance or change them, and also like Williams, he explains how his form of verse—free verse—is difficult to understand. (We must remember that at this time, New Critics emphasized "the art of treating the line" [Williams, *Selected Essays* 277], and, to many poets and critics, free verse was out of vogue). In 1952, Allen Tate attacked Carl Sandburg in the *Saturday Review* for saying in 1940 that T. S. Eliot was close to the Fascists. In 1953, Hayden Carruth reviewed what would be Carl Sandburg's last major work, his autobiography titled *Always the Young Strangers* (1953). Carruth notes the bad grammar, formlessness, "unfeeling use of language," and "appalling juxtapositions" in this "roundtable and sometimes vexatious memoir" (82).

By this time, of course, Carl Sandburg had achieved impressive national fame and had enjoyed the status of American celebrity of sorts since the early 1920s. In 1953, Carl Sandburg appeared on NBC television, and in 1959—at the age of eighty—he was invited to participate in the first nonstop passenger flight across the United States. Events like these only deepened resentment of Sandburg by his contemporaries. His final publication—a short book of poetry—appeared in 1963. Numerous critics reviewed the book. Eight reviews offered damning assessments; only two found a redeeming quality in Sandburg's poetry. Two significant and notable issues about these reviews should be underscored: first, the reviews are unforgiving in their chastisements of Sandburg, and, second, the reviews are written as comprehensive overviews of Sandburg's writing career.

For example, an anonymous review that appeared in the 1963 issue of the *Virginia Quarterly* argues that though "one can hear the voice of their maker, the affirmer, the accepter, the man of age and wisdom [in these new poems they] lack just what almost the whole of Sandburg's poetry lacks—a particular life of its own … [The poems] are really cliches" (qtd. in Salwak 104)). Randall Jarrell's "Fifty Years of American Poetry," published in the *Prairie Schooner* of that same year, calls Sandburg's poems "improvisations whose wording is approximate" (qtd. in Salwak 105). He adds that Sandburg is a very American writer who "sings more stylishly than he writes" and "recites his poems better than they are written" (105). Somner Sorenson's "Poets New and Old: Reviews of Ammons and Sandburg" (1965) in *Discourse: A Review of the Liberal Arts*, states that "half the poems [in *Honey and Salt*] do not merit any serious consideration" (143). Sorenson goes on to say that although Sandburg shows "moments of greatness, the total effect is marred by many inferior poems" (145).

What is most frustrating for Sandburg scholars and, at the same time, equally surprising and puzzling, is the fact that for every article critiquing him, and there are many, there are always several articles defending him. And this is really the only observable trend. Of course, one significant point to be made deals with the persistent level of interest in Sandburg through 1985. Since 1950, the number of articles, book reviews, and discussions in chapters on him in books that treat American literature break down as follows:

1950: Twenty-five		1978: Twenty-one	
1951: Sixteen		1979: Sixteen	
1952: Thirty-nine		1980: Eleven	
1953: Forty		1981: Nine	
1954: Seventeen		1982: Eight	
1955: Sixteen		1983: Eleven	
1956: Ten		1984: Twelve	
1957: Thirteen		1985: Eight	
1958: Thirteen		1986: One	
1959: Seventeen		1987: Five	
1960: Twenty-two		1988: Five	
1961: Fifteen		1989: None	
1962: Eleven		1990: One	
1963: Twenty-four		1991: Two	
1964: Eleven		1992: Four	
1965: Five		1993: One	
1966: Twelve		1994: Four	
1967: Twenty-six		1995: Three	
1968: Forty-eight		1996: Two	
1969: Fifteen		1997: One	
1970: Seventeen		1998: None	
1971: Ten		1999: One	
1972: Six		2000: None	
1973: Eleven		2001: Three	
1974: Five		2002: One	
1975: Nine		2003: Two	
1976: Sixteen		2004: One	
1977: Eleven			

Taking a look at this list, it is easy to see a sharp drop off in interest in Sandburg that began in the early 1980s. Louis Rubin's article "Not to Forget Carl Sandburg. ..." (1977), published in the *Sewanee Review*, speculates about what has happened to Carl Sandburg, Edgar Lee Masters, and Vachel Lindsay. Rubin, like many other critics, noticed that by 1978 there was lackluster interest in Sandburg. Rubin, interestingly, positions Sandburg as a member of a group, which has often been referred to as the "Chicago trio" or the "trio of the Mid-West," and he wants to see all three writers rescued from their literary neglect (Rubin 181).

Many of the critics who support Sandburg specifically respond to the charges registered against him. For example, Daniel Hoffman's "'Moonlight Draws no Mittens': Carl Sandburg Reconsidered" (1978), published in the *Georgia Review*, defends Sandburg's work and style specifically against the criticism of William Carlos Williams. In 1978, Karl Shapiro suggested in the *Chicago Tribune* that Carl Sandburg is now "America's most official poet" (qtd. in Salwak 139) and argued that Sandburg's influence on contemporary poetry was certainly equal to that of Pound and Williams.

By 1978, many scholars of American literature were already exploring—at great length—the reasons why Carl Sandburg's reputation was fading. For example, Paul Ferlazzo's "The Popular Writer, Professors, and the Making of a Reputation: The Case of Carl Sandburg" (1979), published in *Mid America VI*, noted that Sandburg was taught in high schools but ignored altogether in colleges. He argued that professors and literary critics have not conceded greatness to him because of his popularity, his social philosophy, and "the long reign ... of the New Critics" (74).

By 1980, Sandburg's politics once again became central to assessments of him and his work. Interestingly, the famous (or infamous) 1951 William Carlos Williams review of Sandburg's *Complete Poems* resurfaced. Peter Jones's entry in *Reader's Guide to Fifty American Poets* (1980) reviews Sandburg's life and work and sees him as "a radical in poetry and politics" (116), arguing that Sandburg was "always compromised" in his subject matter (116). Jones goes on to quote rather heavily from the 1951 Williams review of Sandburg. In 1984, Genevieve Stuttaford published an article in *Publisher's Weekly* evaluating Sandburg's posthumous book *Ever the Winds of Chance* (1983) and explained how "The book reveals the inner turbulence of the young poet and Socialist and describes the many forces that helped to shape his life and career" (50).

Though Sandburg scholarship is appearing with less frequency, the few discussions that have appeared since 1990 tend to focus on either *Chicago Poems* or *The People, Yes*. No other texts have remained central in Sandburg scholarship. For example, Brian Reed's "Carl Sandburg's 'The People, Yes,' Thirties, Modernism, and the Problem of Bad Political Poetry" (2004) states that Sandburg's

> verse in *The People, Yes* is rather egregious. Egregious, though, not only when held up to the standards of, say, Seamus Heaney or Jorie Graham, but also, crucially, when measured by a pre-World War II audience's sense of what lyric poetry should be. Yes, Sandburg's language is degraded,

> demotic, clunky. So too, he would reply, is public language itself. Fighting for a subjective space apart from the pervasive, invasive discourses of the media and the market is a pyrrhic battle. (184)

Like most critics who have written about Sandburg in the last twenty years, Reed not only cites a damning criticism written of his 1948 novel titled *Remembrance Rock* written by Perry Miller in the *New York Times Book Review,* but he also revisits the 1951 review of *Complete Poems* written by William Carlos Williams. Reed makes clear that

> after this public dressing-down by a fellow modernist, the remainder of the 1950s saw a swift decline in Sandburg's representation in anthologies and textbooks. He virtually ceased to receive extended critical commentary ... The fall from grace was so dramatic, so final, that its inaugural shove is worth examining in some detail. (Reed 187)

Although Reed does not explore this "inaugural shove" in great detail, he does explain how

> the powerful, formalist-leaning literary circles already inclined to challenge Sandburg's pre-World War II stature and authority—those circles that had savaged *Remembrance Rock*—seized upon Williams's thesis. After 1951, Sandburg's academic reputation was cemented as the author of a handful of sincere but clumsy 1910s lyrics best appreciated by readers uneducated in subtleties of form, technique, and tone. When his post-1920s work surfaces in criticism after mid-century, it almost always does so as a strawman ... (189)

In fact, the years after 1920 were Sandburg's most critical "political" years—years when he was giving voice and shape to a more complex political ideology. And it must be emphasized that this is the most prolific and mature period of Sandburg's literary career, and therefore deserves a careful and accurate assessment. Understanding his political project in his post-1920 works is vital to an accurate understanding of Carl Sandburg.

Chapter 4

Carl Sandburg's New Imagination and Project of Nation-Building

Sandburg's Nation-Building: "I Wanted Something More in the American Lingo. I Was Tired of Princes and Princesses and I Sought the American Equivalent of Elves and Gnomes."
—Carl Sandburg quoted in *Carl Sandburg: A Biography* (Niven 389)

In 1922, Sandburg said, "In the making of books [of poetry] I've reached the peak and the breaking point ... They've got my best blood and heartbeats and breath" (Niven 388). A period of change would manifest itself with great force in the works that would immediately follow.

1922 is a very significant year in helping to understand Sandburg's shifting perception of himself and his role as a writer. By this time, he had already published four volumes of poetry, *Chicago Poems, Cornhuskers, Smoke and Steel*, and *Slabs of the Sunburnt West*, and in the literary world of the Sunburnt West, he initiated a period of dramatic artistic experimentation and complexity—a complexity that most critical assessments have almost entirely overlooked. Furthermore, in 1922 Sandburg began broadening his artistic interests, and he broke out of his narrow concept of his role as an artist, one that had identified him as a poet who doubled as a social critic.

In addition, 1922 marks the initiation of a new project in Sandburg's works, one of nation-building. From this point onward, Carl Sandburg transforms into, and presents himself as, an American patriot. His many works, in multiple genres, served as efforts to give Americans of all ages a sense of their country's history as well as its potential. He also wanted Americans to understand and appreciate the common man and the common laborer. It is important to underscore that between 1904 and 1922 Sandburg had almost exclusively restricted himself to writing poetry and journalism, but in 1922 he discovered the great potential of other genres, including children's books, adult and juvenile biographies, and songbooks. This year marks the beginning of a new epoch in Sandburg's literary journey.

In his Introduction to the 1990 Edition of Carl Sandburg's *The American Songbag*, which was initially published in 1927, Garrison Keillor describes Sandburg's status as a literary man in 1922. Keillor explains that by this time, Sandburg was a well-published and confident man of letters with a well-established national reputation. Keillor emphasizes how

> in six years [since the publication of *Chicago Poems*] he [Sandburg] had published three volumes of poetry—*Chicago Poems, Cornhuskers, Smoke and Steel*, the best work of his life—and was hard at work on his *Rootabaga Stories* (1922), and the two-volume *Abraham Lincoln: The Prairie Years* (1926) and was assembling *The American Songbag* and pursuing a career as a performing literary man. He was not quite forty. (qtd. in Sandburg, *American Songbag* vii)

Keillor goes on to explain how "As a Lecturer, Sandburg worked schools and colleges, women's clubs, lyceums, and chautauquas for a set fee (by 1921 he was asking $125), but he was sufficiently confident of his drawing power to appear for 50 percent of the receipts (after expenses, with Sandburg handling all the advertising)" (vii). While Keillor points out Sandburg's artistic experimentalism and his interest in becoming a performing man of letters, he overlooks the equally important fact that Carl Sandburg was, indeed, beginning the largest and most ambitious project of his life—the project of nation-building and the project of creating a sense of patriotism in the hearts and minds of Americans of all ages.

Within Sandburg's project of nation-building, we can also see an evolving and extremely complex political ideology in his works—one still deeply rooted in different strands, combinations, cross-pollinations, and complex negotiations of Socialist ideology. This element in Sandburg's post-1922 works, in essence a silent Socialism, makes an assessment of Sandburg more difficult and complicates an analysis of the new imagination at work. The following chapters will touch upon and analyze how Sandburg's political stance manifested itself within the project of nation-building.

The goal of this chapter is to focus and clarify how Carl Sandburg, in various ways, was attempting to reinvent or reconstruct American literature. The literature he produces—in various genres—serves as clear evidence that he began not only to experiment with form but he began stressing different subjects and themes as he attempted to advance his political ideology in a less conspicuous fashion. At times, distinct residual vestiges of Sandburg the radical poet—vestiges which show a deeply political man—can be seen in the children's stories and in every work published thereafter.

For example, his biography of Abraham Lincoln fuses biography with myth-making (this biography was in certain respects *sui generis*, and it was definitely unique among Lincoln biographies). In the tradition of the epic, his novel *Remembrance Rock* (1948) encompasses a sweeping panorama of American history and attempts to reconstruct and resituate our understanding of our past. The few volumes of poetry he brought forth after 1922, *Good Morning, America* (1928), *The People, Yes* (1936), and *Honey and Salt* (1963), were both critical of the social problems plaguing America and extremely optimistic in message, evidence of the potential power and influence Sandburg saw in his works. It is interesting to note how each work displayed a cinematic sensibility. For example, *Good Morning, America* opens with a wide-lens description of world history, and *The People, Yes* presents 107 untitled poems—hinting at an inherent and threaded thematic montage-like cohesiveness in the poems. This was all a part of Sandburg's new creative vision, and these works are the centerpieces that reveal his great experiment.

The most significant factor that contributed to the fueling of this shift in his work came in 1920 when the *Chicago Daily News* added an additional responsibility to his permanent duty as staff reporter, that of film critic. He was to review about six movies every week. (The hundreds of reviews he wrote over this eight-year period have been collected in a book by Arnie Bernstein, with an Introduction by Roger Ebert, titled *"The Movies Are": Carl Sandburg's Film Reviews and Essays, 1920–1928* [2000]. A second book that details this period in Sandburg's life is Dale and Doug Fetherling's *Carl Sandburg at the Movies: A Poet in the Silent Era, 1920–1927* [1985]).

Sandburg made his critical debut on Monday, September 27, 1920—at a time when movies were generally not taken seriously as an art form in most critical circles (Bernstein 4). While the front page of the paper carried stories about "Chicago baseball's Black Sox and the 1919 World Series fix" (Bernstein 1), Sandburg's first review examined *Hitchin' Posts*, a now-forgotten Western starring Frank Mayo. He immediately became a passionate film advocate, and

> true to his other writing Sandburg was no snob, finding value in all kinds of movies. He loved the psychological depth of director Erich von Stroheim and the formula shoot-'em-up adventures of cowboy star Buck Jones. Sandburg felt equally at home extolling the virtues of artistic European movies as he did in recommending novelty films featuring all-canine or all-monkey casts. He once compared the moody cinematography of a Rin-Tin-Tin picture to that of the German Expressionist classic *The Cabinet of Dr. Caligari*. In his seven and one half years as the "cinema

expert," Sandburg developed a distinctive critical voice that ultimately complements his better-known work. (Bernstein 4)

Throughout these years as film critic, Sandburg was impressed by developments in film technology, dutifully reporting on new cinematic breakthroughs in color, sound, and other innovations, including three-dimensional movies and motion pictures for the blind. In addition, he "constantly exhorted filmmakers to push their creative talents and challenge audiences with intelligent work" (Bernstein 2). As an artist, he would hold himself to this high standard as well.

In addition, his reviews, often no more than two-hundred words in length, are never disparaging, and reveal Sandburg's keen eye for technological advancements. His November 14, 1923, review of Buster Keaton's *The Three Ages* is a good example that reveals how sensitive his eye was to technological experimentation. He says in his review:

> The film is notable as one of the first features to incorporate live action with animation. Keaton's entrance in the first segment, as a caveman riding on a dinosaur, was created as an in-camera special effect. First the comic actor was photographed against a white background on the upper portion of the film frame. The film was then rewound in the camera and an animated dinosaur was added beneath Keaton. (Bernstein 8)

Sandburg's attention to detail and interest in the technology of overlaying images helped to further nurture and develop his own creative imagination. This manifests itself with great force in his children's stories and in his biography of Abraham Lincoln, *Abraham Lincoln: The Prairie Years*, which were written concurrently.

A closer study of this same review foreshadows Sandburg's literary techniques in virtually all of the works he published after 1920. Sandburg writes:

> Taking his [Buster Keaton] cue from the more serious pictures, on which this is a burlesque, the opening reel has a book with a title shown, and the cover is opened as though we are all anxious to read the book, and then two or three pages of reading come along, as though we are going to settle down to a lesson in history and instruction with regard to how civilization rose out of the dark days of savagery. (Bernstein 8)

The realization that movies could offer "a lesson in history and instruction with regard to how civilization rose out of the dark days of savagery" challenged Sandburg to produce the same kind of works. This interest in the possibility of "retelling," "reconstructing," or "resituating" the past gave Sandburg a new template for his own works of biography and poetry, as well as fiction for children and adults.

In 1925 Sandburg reviewed movies like *Seven Chances*, another Buster Keaton film, pointing out the hilarity of the story, and in 1927, he reviewed *The General*, which "is based upon historical fact and treats in a lighter vein an incident during the Civil War known as 'the Andrews railroad raid,' which occurred in 1862 when a band of Union soldiers invaded Confederate territory and captured 'The General,' one of the south's crack railroad engines" (Bernstein 7). In this movie, Sandburg saw the "hilarity, pathos, and thrills," but he also recognized its epic quality. Movies like these provided him with the model he could follow as he began projecting his own works through this imaginative prism.

Seeing experimentation on the big screen inspired a new literary experimentation in his work. In essence, the movies he saw encouraged and fueled his new imagination. Penelope Niven explains how:

> The convergence of the motion picture, folk music, travel, home life, and the often preposterous realities of daily news events helped to shape *Slabs of the Sunburnt West* (1922). There was an overlay of new imagery, drawn, most likely unconsciously, from the realm of the motion picture. Immersed as he was in a weekly round of films, Sandburg inevitably drew images from the new form into his work. In addition to watching at least six movies a week, he wrote background pieces to feed the avid American appetite for backstage details about the production of movies, and the private lives of producers, directors, and stars. Thus the motion picture was one of the dominant forces at work in Sandburg's imagination during the decade of the twenties. (Niven 389)

His film reviews led to an increased awareness of the varied audiences attending these movies and he was an eyewitness to the profound effect these movies had on them. No doubt this prompted Sandburg to reevaluate his own role as a writer. Furthermore, Sandburg "immediately saw the far-reaching value of motion picture newsreels, which brought the American people close-ups of 'History in the making'" (Niven 403).

If movies could reach mass audiences, why not books? Could his books create the same effect as these moving pictures? Could his books reach a broader audience, or maybe even different audiences? And was there a way to transform existing traditions governing different genres?

Chapter 5

Sandburg's New Imagination: The Children's Books and Rootabaga Country

W e thus see a new Carl Sandburg at work in his two children's books, published subsequently in 1922 and 1923, in which he created a fictive Rootabaga Country. (Sandburg changed the spelling from rutabaga "perhaps to Americanize it, or to emphasize its basic meaning" [Niven 389].) Paula Sandburg, Carl's wife, recognized his urge to transform the genre of children's stories when she explained how

> Carl thought that American children should have something different, more suited to their ideals and surroundings. So his stories did not concern knights on white chargers, but simple people, such as Potato Face Blind Man who played the accordion, the White Horse Girl and the Blue Wind Boy, or commonplace objects, a rag doll and a broom handle, a knife and fork. (qtd. in Niven 389–90)

Niven adds that "The fairy-tale escapades of the Roaring Twenties were just beginning, but fairy tales in those immediate post-war years were few and far between. Into that unlikely setting, Sandburg introduced his *Rootabaga Stories*" (389).

To better appreciate Carl Sandburg's works at this time, it is important to contextualize the America for which Carl Sandburg was writing. U.S. participation in World War I had marked a crucial stage in the nation's evolution as a world power: "More narrowly but more immediately, it involved American artists and thinkers with the brutal actualities of large-scale modern war, so different from imaginary heroism" (Baym 939). The sense of a great civilization being destroyed, of social breakdown, and of individual powerlessness became part of the American experience as a result of the nation's participation in World War I. It is important to note that Carl Sandburg, almost single-handedly, used literature to combat—not expose or further manifest—this sense of cultural and moral collapse. In this lies his project of nation-building. To illustrate the point,

Sandburg's sense of the design and aim of his first Lincoln biography, which he was working on diligently at the time he was writing his children's stories, reveals that he conscientiously believed that "Perhaps poetry, art, human behavior in this country, which has need to build on it own traditions, would be served by a life of Lincoln stressing the fifty-two years previous to his Presidency" (Niven 415).

Sandburg also believed that

> Lincoln's personal history was a prism through which much of the nation's own growth could be viewed, Sandburg believed, for Lincoln was a product of his era. The "inside changes" working in Lincoln were connected to "the changes developing in the heart and mind of the country." Lincoln was irrevocably bound to his times, destined to be the spokesman for his countrymen and their rapidly changing national life. Lincoln was "lawyer, politician, a good neighbor and storyteller, a live, companionable man; these belonged to his role. He was to be a mind, a spirit, a tongue and voice." (Niven 415)

But it was not only the Lincoln biography that would contribute to this project of what can be seen as "nation-building." Every work from 1922 forward served this function in some way. Sandburg's aim as a writer would become much more complex than in the years 1916–1920. In these earlier years he had made an effort to expose social and economic inequalities and was directly promoting the benefits of Socialism and the ideology of the Industrial Workers of the World (IWW). After 1922, he saw himself, much like Walt Whitman, as the true voice of the people, and his over-arching message was one of optimism, hope, and promise.

At a time when many expatriates were taking up residence in Paris—writers like Gertrude Stein, Sylvia Beach, Ezra Pound, Ernest Hemingway, Djuna Barnes, Kay Boyle, E. E. Cummings, Hilda Doolittle, Janet Flanner, Glenway Wescott, Archibald MacLeish, and F. Scott Fitzgerald—Carl Sandburg chose to stay in America. At a time when scores of anti-war and anti-America novels were being published—works which include John Dos Passos's *Three Soldiers* (1921) E. E. Cummings's *The Enormous Room* (1922), Thomas Boyd's *Through the Wheat* (1923), and Ernest Hemingway's *The Sun Also Rises* (1926) and *A Farewell to Arms* (1929)—Carl Sandburg was, instead, celebrating America. He was celebrating its accomplishments, its might, and its potential as a country poised for even further industrial and technological progress. There was nothing anti-American about Carl Sandburg after 1922. There was also nothing defensive or insular about him either.

The two monumental literary works published in 1922—James Joyce's *Ulysses* and T. S. Eliot's "The Waste Land"—were representative modernist products. At the heart of the modernist aesthetic lay the conviction that the "previously sustaining structures of human life, whether social, political, religious, or artistic, had been either destroyed or shown up to be falsehoods or fantasies" (Baym 944). In his own way, Sandburg was reacting to the same pressures. But instead of offering a bleak and pessimistic view of life and human nature, Sandburg's works make an attempt to offer common readers a renewed sense of optimism. Instead of participating in the modernist tradition of writing obfuscating and challenging fragmented texts, Sandburg offers tightly knitted works that clearly contain over-arching themes of hope and promise. In many ways, Carl Sandburg took it upon himself to put back together a country that many writers saw as hopelessly fragmented.

In the opening poem of *Slabs of the Sunburnt West* (1922), "The Windy City," Sandburg writes:

> The lean hands of wagon men
> put out pointing fingers here,
> Picked this crossway, put it on a map,
> Set up their sawbucks, fixed shotguns,
> Found a hitching place for the pony express,
> Made a hitching place for the iron horse,
> The one-eyed horse with the fire-spit head,
> Found a homelike spot and said, "Make a home,"
> Saw this corner with a mesh of rails, shuttling
> People, shunting cars, shaping the junk of
> The earth to a new city.
> The hands of men took hold and tugged
> And the breaths of men went into the junk
>
> And the junk stood up into the skyscrapers and asked:
>
> Who am I? Am I a city? And if I am what is my name?
> And once while the time whistles blew and blew again
> The men answered: Long ago we gave you a name,
> Long ago we laughed and said: You? Your name is Chicago.
> [...]
> So between the Great Lakes,
> The Grand De Tour, and the Grand Prairie,
> The living lighted skyscrapers stand,
> Spotting the blue dusk with checkers of yellow,

> Streamers of smoke and silver,
> Parallelograms of night-gray watchmen,
> Singing a soft moaning song: I am a child,
> a belonging. (*Complete Poems* 271–72)

In many ways, the style of this poem is representative of previously published poems found in *Cornhuskers* (1918) and *Smoke and Steel* (1920). However, what is different about this poem is its broad scope and immense breadth; much like the epic movies he was reviewing for his column, Sandburg began using his poetry to resituate the past by pointing out the splendor of Western expansion and Manifest Destiny. Like never before, many of the poems in this volume, as well as those published thereafter, attempt to retell American history, and this was done to give Americans pride and a renewed sense of understanding of their native land. In *Slabs of the Sunburn West*, Sandburg is more creative and more American than he had ever been.

The second poem in the volume, "Washington Monument by Night," contains lines like these: "The republic is a dream./Nothing happens unless first a dream" (10–11) and "The wind bit hard at Valley Forge one Christmas./Soldiers tied rags on their feet" (12–13). From this volume of poetry onward, Sandburg would use his literature in a boldly ambitious way—he would use it as a way to build up the nation's consciousness of its own past and as a vehicle to resituate and re-present the nation's rich history, one founded on idealism. Each piece would be framed in such a way that would allow Sandburg to take a sweeping, panoramic view of America's past, present, and future. Already in his mid-forties, Carl Sandburg began the project of nation-building, and he would continue to work on it for the next forty-five years. He began with the children in this country, believing that their collective consciousness could be altered.

In his biography, *Carl Sandburg: His Life and Works* (1987), North Callahan comments on the children's stories Sandburg produced and explains how he believes the "delightful tales demonstrate more than anything else the originality and remarkable versatility of Carl Sandburg. Here was a man who could change from the heavy rhythms of Walt Whitman and the tragic story of Abraham Lincoln to a whimsical never-never land of children" (105). Sandburg had read the fairy tales of Hans Christian Andersen, the Danish writer of fairy tales, poetry, novels, and dramas, but said he could find no equivalent in American literature (Callahan 105). He would be the American Hans Christian Andersen.

Rootabaga Stories (1922) is a unique work for many reasons. Primarily, though, it is a touchstone work for Sandburg because it was written and published at a time when children's stories had no "geographic reality" (Golden 222). Harry Golden, a close friend of Sandburg and author of the biography *Carl Sandburg* (1961), explains how

> Rootabaga Country is an American country. It has a railroad, ragpickers, policemen, ball teams, tall grass. It is mapped out. If it existed, you could get to it and find your way around. Geographic reality is what makes the *Rootabaga Stories* the first genuinely American fairy tales. The stories are fairy tales because the population of Rootabaga Country does not know about social distinction (although they differ from one another); and because they do not have money (although Potato Bug Millionaire collects fleems). The stories are American in diction, in foolishness, in fancy, and American in place.
>
> Thus, Rootabaga Country is more than a fairy tale. Rootabaga Country is Carl Sandburg's Main Street, his Yoknapatawpha County, his Gibbsville, Pennsylvania.
>
> Rootabaga Country (like Galesburg, Illinois, itself) is a good place to live because of the people who inhabit it. Sandburg never fell for the temptation to seize upon this aspect—life in the small town—and use it for ridicule, and do what so many other of our writers have done to point out the dullness and narrowness of the lives and interests of the people. Sinclair Lewis set the fashion with *Main Street*, Sherwood Anderson in *Winesburg, Ohio*, Phil Stong in *Village Tale*, and James Gould Cozzens in *The Last Adam*. (Golden 222–223)
>
> [...]
>
> The citizens of Gopher Prairie [in *Main Street*] "had lost the power of play as well as the power of impersonal thought." One of Lewis's more sympathetic residents speculates: "I wonder if the small town isn't, with some lovely exceptions, a social appendix? Some day these dull market towns may be as obsolete as monasteries."
>
> It is exactly the power of play and the power of impersonal thought that the citizens of Rootabaga Country will not give up. (Golden 222–24)

In addition, what set Sandburg apart from other authors of children's stories was that he did relatively little overt moralizing. Also, Sandburg's *Rootabaga Stories* "are largely free of [the] violence typical of most fairy tales" (Niven 391). Penelope Niven adds that

> after years of reporting fact and circumstance, Sandburg found welcome liberation in the country he created. There he could invent language,

> geography, customs and people, garbed in fun and nonsense, and move them through adventures masked in whimsy but, in many instances, firmly grounded in the reality he sought to leave behind. He discovered he could tell more of the truth in his fictions for children than he could tell in the often hostile world of realities. (Niven 394)

Even though the stories seem to have a disarming simplicity, their scope and breadth is important to examine.

The stories in *Rootabaga Stories* can be divided into two categories. The first is the whimsical—the story that seems to consist of unrestrained imagination and play, evidence of a new fancy in Sandburg's works never seen before. However, even these stories often contain a very serious subtext that can be easily discerned by more mature readers. The second category is the story that seems to offer some type of social critique, the story that seems to be intricately woven with "strands of events of the times" (Niven 388)—residual evidence of a deeply political and radical poet.

A good example of the first type of story can be seen in "How the Five Rusty Rats Helped Find A New Village." In the story,

> The people who ate Cream Puffs came together and met in the streets and picked up their belongings on their shoulders and marched out of the Village of Liver-and-Onions saying, "We shall find a new place for a village and the name of it shall be the Village of Cream Puffs."
>
> They marched out on the prairie with their baggage and belongings in sacks on their shoulders. And a blizzard came up. Snow filled the sky. The wind blew and made a noise like heavy wagon axles grinding and crying. (32–3)

As the story continues, the snow continues falling "all day and all night and all the next day." And just when the travelers are about to give up hope, "five lucky rats came, the five rusty rats, rust on their skin and hair, rust on their feet and noses, rust all over, and especially, most especially of all, rust on their long curved tails" (33). The rats invite these people to take hold of their tails and lead them to safety, and, eventually, to the place where "the Village of Cream Puffs now stands" (36).

A similar story is titled "The Two Skyscrapers Who Decided to Have a Child." The story begins with a description of "Two skyscrapers [that] stood across the street from each other in the Village of Liver-and-Onions. In the daylight when the streets poured full of people buying and selling, these two skyscrapers talked with each other the same as mountains talk" (133). Eventually, after months of talking and "leaning towards each other and whispering in the night the same as mountains lean and whisper in the night" (134), the two skyscrapers decided to have a child:

> "It must be a free child," they said to each other. "It must not be a child standing still all its life on a street corner. Yes, if we have a child she must be free to run across the prairie, to the mountains, to the sea. Yes, it must be a free child."
>
> So time passed on. Their child came. It was a railroad train, the Golden Spike Limited, the fastest long distance train in the Rootabaga Country. It ran across the prairie, to the mountains, to the sea. (137)

The train would carry "a thousand people a thousand miles a day" (138). Eventually, though, it crashed and many lives were lost. The story ends abruptly. This story is highly imaginative but it is also a good example of Sandburg's participation in literary trends of the modernist works of the time because it "ends without resolution" (Baym 944).

However, other tales in Sandburg's *Rootabaga Stories* serve as scathing criticisms and indictments of American society, and although he uses characters and plots to carefully disguise his criticisms, the message still comes through.

For example, in "The Dollar Watch and the Five Jack Rabbits" Sandburg introduces readers to two characters traveling across Rootabaga Country; they meet a man in a town who looked sad. They ask him why he was sad and he explains how his brother is in jail. When they ask him why, he explains how his

> brother put on a straw hat in the middle of the winter and went out on the streets laughing; my brother had his hair cut pompompadour and went out on the streets bareheaded in the summertime laughing; and these things were against the law. Worst of all he sneezed at the wrong time and he sneezed in front of the wrong persons; he sneezed when it was not wise to sneeze. So he will be hanged tomorrow. (143)

As the story continues, readers learn that just before this young man is about to be hanged, he "uses his fingers winding up the watch and pushing on the stem winder [and] the dollar watch changed into a dragon fly ship and [he] flew away before anybody could stop him" (144). Stories like these serve as disarmingly simple, fictional allegories to make children think about social inequalities and the dangers of accepted social mores.

We should keep in mind that Carl Sandburg's *The Chicago Race Riots, July, 1919* examined a very similar kind of tension in society that was founded on racism. A

1920 letter Sandburg wrote to John A. Lomax, who helped to establish the Library of Congress Folk Music Archives, articulates Sandburg's views on segregation:

> I know you would understand, if we had the time to go over all the evidence, that there is a prejudice which if it could achieve its desire would segregate, repress, and again make a chattel of the Negro if that status could again be restored. Both north and south this prejudice was loosened with the end of the war and was given added impetus by the very physical hysteria of war. I believe that this prejudice, as sheer prejudice, runs deeper and wider down south than up north and that this is the basic reason why the southern business interests have completely failed in their endeavors to induce movements of Negro population from northern points back south again. There is no place in the south that I have heard of where the negro has the freedom of ballot and the political equality and economic opportunity accorded him in Chicago and other northern cities. ... (qtd. in Mitgang 176)

We must remember that Jim Crow Laws were firmly in place at this time. These laws enforced racial segregation and discrimination throughout the country, especially in the South, from the late nineteenth century to the 1960s. These laws were a fact of life, and so were lynchings. In a story like "The Dollar Watch and the Five Jack Rabbits," it seems likely that Sandburg was alluding to Jim Crow Laws and the lynchings taking place across the country.

In *Rootabaga Stories*, we also meet Young Leather and Red Slippers who come to a new town where they see

> a skyscraper higher than all the other skyscrapers. A rich man dying wanted to be remembered and left in his last will and testament a command that they should build a building so high it would scrape the thunder clouds and stand higher than all other skyscrapers with his name carved in stone letters on the top of it, and an electric sign at night with his name on it, and a clock on the tower with his name on it.
> "I am hungry to be remembered and have my name spoken by many people after I am dead," the rich man told his friends. "I command you, therefore, to throw the building high in the air because the higher it goes the longer I will be remembered and the longer the years men will mention my name after I am dead." (145–46)

This is a very peculiar passage because, again, it seems to clearly resemble real events of the times, events with which any living American adult could connect. Sandburg himself explains in a personal letter to Negley Cochran in 1926:

> The big fact for me about Woolworth is that when at last he had topped his ambition to have the biggest building in the world, he used to walk around it every morning, ride to the top and down, and again walk around it wondering what it was all about. While with Bill Wrigley the big fact is that he wanted his poor goddamn name spelled on the tower-clock instead of the hour numbers. ... (qtd. in Mitgang 239)

This story perfectly illustrates how Sandburg injected political ideology into his works and it showcases the selfish and narcissistic characteristics of the most privileged economic class in American society. Of course, in his children's stories, specific names are withheld, but in the poems they are not.

Not surprisingly, Carl Sandburg's *Good Morning, America* (1928) includes a poem titled "Again?"—which directly echoes this very story of "a rich man":

> Old Man Woolworth put up a building.
> There it was; his dream; all true;
> The biggest building in the world.
> Babel, the Ninevah Hanging Gardens,
> Karnak, all old, outclassed.
> And now, here at last, what of it?
> What about it? Well, every morning
> We'll walk around it and look up.
> And every morning we'll ask what
> It means and where it's going. ...
> (*Complete Poems* 368)

It was children's stories like the one about "Old Man Woolworth" that prompted criticism from young and old readers alike. North Callahan explains how

> Evidently there was one young person who was unsure as to what he [Sandburg] meant in these stories [*Rootabaga Stories* and *Rootabaga Pigeons*]. From Providence, Rhode Island, came the following letter: "Dear Mr. Sandburg, I am a junior at the Lincoln School and as one of our English assignments we are to write on an American author. Since I have chosen you as my subject I feel that I must ask you the following questions. I have been reading your *Rootabaga Stories* for the first time and to be perfectly frank do not really find their point. I see a good deal of satire and feel that it shows peoples' dissatisfaction with what exists in life. Am I correct in assuming this? If this is true then did you intend the *Rootabaga Stories* for adolescents and adults as well as for children? Sincerely, Ann Adams." (Callahan, *Carl Sandburg* 110)

Sandburg never replied to this letter, but he knew that an army of critics would point out similar concerns. Again, this letter supports the idea that vestiges of a political and radical Sandburg survived into his post-1922 writings, and it helps to complicate our understanding of his project of nation-building.

Stories like "How Bimbo the Snip's Thumb Stuck to His Nose when the Wind Changed" also seem to be layered with elements that seem a bit above the intellect of young readers. This story tells the tale of a young boy who "put [his] thumb to his nose and wiggled [his] fingers at the iceman when the wind changed. And just like mother always said, if the wind changed the thumb would stay fastened to [his] nose and not come off" (124). As Bimbo the Snip attempts to look for help, he encounters an

> old widow woman whose husband had been killed in a sewer explosion when he was digging sewer ditches. And the old woman was carrying a bundle of picked-up kindling wood in a bag on her back because she did not have money enough to buy coal.
>
> Bevo the Hike told her, "You have troubles. So have I. You are carrying a load on your back people can see. I am carrying a load and nobody sees it." (126)

This passage, again, seems to echo the earlier, more militant Sandburg that readers encountered in *Chicago Poems*, where he explored the bitter relationship that existed between workers and company owners.

The second type of narrative dominates this volume of short stories. Perhaps because the book is wide in its breadth and scope and strengths and is layered with both fantasy and fact, the volume was enormously successful with young readers. As a matter of fact, it was this volume that made Sandburg a wealthy man, and his publisher, Harcourt, encouraged Sandburg to create a sequel that would appear several months later.

Rootabaga Pigeons (1923), the sequel to *Rootabaga Stories*, was equally successful. Again, many of the stories in this highly imaginative book—loosely connected via several characters, namely Blixie Bimber and Potato Face Blind Man—contain elements which are both serious and light-hearted. For example, in the story titled "How Bozo the Button Buster Busted All His Buttons When a Mouse Came" explains how

> Bozo had buttons all over him. The buttons on Bozo fitted so tight, and there were so many buttons, that sometimes when he took his lungs full of new wind to go on talking a button would bust loose and fly into the

face of whoever he was speaking to. Sometimes when he took new wind into his lungs two buttons would bust loose and fly into the faces of two people he was speaking to.

Now, you must understand, Bozo was different from other people. He had a string tied to him. It was a long string hanging down with a knot at the end. He used to say, "Sometimes I forget where I am; then I feel for the string tied to me, and I follow the string to where it is tied to me; then I know where I am again." (Sandburg, *Sandburg Range* 104)

This disarmingly simple story—like so many other stories in *Rootabaga Pigeons*—evolves into a very abstract story. Bozo the Button Buster, on his last day in the Village of Cream Puffs, "stood in the public square and he was all covered with buttons, more buttons than ever before, and all the buttons fitting tight, and five, six buttons busting loose and flying into the air whenever he took his lungs full of wind to go on speaking" (105). He begins a long monologue that is worth repeating here:

"When the sky began to fall, who was it ran out and held up the sky?" he sang out. "It was me, it was me ran out and held up the sky when the sky began to fall."

"When the blue came off the sky, where did they get the blue to put on the sky to make it blue again? It was me, it was me picked the bluebirds and the blue pigeons to get the blue to fix the sky."

"When it rains now it rains umbrellas first so everybody has an umbrella for the rain afterward. Who fixed that? I did – Bozo the Button Buster."

[...]

"Who took the salt out of the sea and put it back again? Who took the fishes out of the sea and put them back again? That was me."

All the time Bozo kept on speaking the buttons kept on busting because he had to stop so often to fill his lungs with new wind to go on speaking. The public square was filled with piles of buttons that kept busting off from Bozo the Button Buster that day.

And at last a mouse came, a sneaking, slippery, quick little mouse. He ran with a flash to the string tied to Bozo, the long string hanging down with a knot in the end. He bit the knot and cut it loose. He slit the string with his teeth as Bozo cried, "Ai! Ai! Ai!"

The last of all the buttons busted loose off Bozo. The clothes fell off. The people came up to see what was happening to Bozo. There was nothing in the clothes. The man inside the clothes was gone. All that was left was buttons and a few clothes. (104)

Examining a work like "How Bozo the Button Buster Busted All His Buttons When a Mouse Came" helps us understand why Sandburg's stories were given mixed reviews. For example, Mabel H. B. Mussey wrote a review of *Rootabaga Stories* in the *Nation* in December of 1922 and argued that "no intelligent child could make much sense of this collection" (Mussey 618). Muna Lee reviewed the same volume in January of 1923 in the *Double Dealer* and explained how Sandburg's "stories vary greatly in mood. Some are unnecessarily harrowing for a child's imagination. His fairy tales strictly have proletarian fairies" (Lee 38).

M. G. Bonner concluded the opposite though. In the November 23, 1923, *International Book Review,* he offered the following evaluation: "This is close to the work of a genius, although some of the writing is 'uneven.' It is as though Carl Sandburg brushed aside every old idea upon which to build a story and proceeded to make his own out of new materials which he had discovered" (qtd. in Salwak 16). This point underscores Sandburg's plan to sketch out a book of children's stories containing no kings and queens; instead, these were common people, some marginalized members of society, but this plan to introduce young readers to common people was the foundation of Carl Sandburg's project of nation-building. All of Sandburg's works published after 1922, like those before, focused on and celebrated the common man.

Ultimately, Sandburg's children's stories were highly imaginative language experiments, but it is important to note that the residual political themes that were so conspicuous in his previous works of poetry still managed to find their way into these juvenile books. From this moment forward, though, it was clear that Sandburg's juvenile literature—with a great deal more to come—would be highly experimental as it loosely cross-pollinated the creative imagination with events of the time. The goal, though, was one of nation-building. This project would manifest itself with even greater force in subsequent works as he looked to a figure from the American past.

Chapter 6

A Hero for America's Children: Abe Lincoln Grows Up

From Walt Whitman, Carl Sandburg had taken a deep and profound interest in Abraham Lincoln:

> Since boyhood, [Sandburg] had admired Lincoln. He had grown up listening to the talk of people who saw Lincoln with their own eyes, and heard him speak. Galesburg [Sandburg's hometown] was full of Lincoln history. Sandburg and Harcourt [his publisher] began to talk about a biography, four hundred pages long, written in simple language for young people, concentrating on Lincoln's prairie boyhood, so much like Sandburg's own. He purchased a ten-volume set of Civil War photographs on December 21, 1922, and several biographies of Lincoln and other Civil War figures. Deliberately, he turned toward the past, embarking on an ambitious exploration of American history. (Niven 407)

After the enormously successful publication of *Abraham Lincoln: The Prairie Years in* 1926, a work which will be discussed in detail later, Sandburg and his publisher, Alfred Harcourt. wanted to publish a version of the biography aimed at younger readers (at this time, no juvenile biography of Lincoln existed). That project soon came to fruition. The biography of Lincoln was extremely unorthodox because

> Most other Lincoln biographies of the nineteenth and early twentieth centuries concentrated on Lincoln's public life, but Sandburg announced his attention to probe the interior, private man, the "illuminated, mysterious personality," the "elusive and dark player on the stage of destiny." He experimented in biography as he did in every genre he tried. His innovative, often unwieldy, sometimes rhapsodic biography of Lincoln would offend and perplex many critics, in part because Sandburg undertook a difficult and unorthodox search for the "silent workings" of Lincoln's inner life. (Niven 415)

Even at that, just as they had with his two children's books, the copies of *Abraham Lincoln: The Prairie Years* flew off the shelf, and Sandburg's publisher, Harcourt, just as he had done with previous volumes, wanted Sandburg to turn the two-volume work into a condensed one-volume edition. This would allow Harcourt to increase his profits in the newly established Book-of-the-Month Club.

In addition, Harcourt encouraged Sandburg to "publish a long excerpt from the early chapters of *Abraham Lincoln: the Prairie Years*, entitle it *Abe Lincoln Grows Up*, and sell it to the juvenile audiences first envisioned for Sandburg's biography" (Niven 461–62). By this time, it is important to consider that Sandburg had established a national reputation as a popular celebrity, and was a well-known figure in American letters.

Also, with the publication of his Rootabaga Series, Sandburg had developed a firm and respectable reputation as a writer of children's books. Published in 1928, *Abe Lincoln Grows Up* received little attention because Sandburg had been publishing prolifically since 1922. As stated earlier, he published *Slabs of the Sunburnt West* in 1922, *Rootabaga Stories* was published that same year, and in 1923 he published *Rootabaga Pigeons*. In 1926, he published the enormously successful and well-received *Abraham Lincoln: the Prairie Years*, in 1927 *The American Songbag*, and in 1928 *Good Morning, America* as well as *Abe Lincoln Grows Up*.

Carl Sandburg distilled the contents for this work, aimed at young readers, from *Abraham Lincoln: The Prairie Years*, and his plan for this new volume—just as it had been in the original—was to present the life of Abraham Lincoln through the larger prism of American history. The possibility of this overlay, or this interest in contextualization, was being modeled for him in the many movies he reviewed. But unlike the earlier children's books published in 1922 and in 1923, the aim of this book was to acquaint young American children with the life and times of a man Sandburg saw as a perfect Socialist because of his "pervasive simplicity of speech and lifestyle; his kindness and generosity; his dislike of all pretense; his humility" (Niven 415). This biography of Lincoln, in a different form than the two volumes of children's stories, represents an escalation of Carl Sandburg's project of nation-building.

Al Benson, the reactionary author of the *Copperhead Chronicle*, accurately, if perversely, recognized why Carl Sandburg, always dutiful and consistent in his Socialist leanings,

> should author a series of books on the socialist icon of the 19th century,
> Abraham Lincoln ... Sandburg had to have been aware of Lincoln's socialist

tendencies and policies and could, no doubt, be in complete sympathy with them, enough so that he would present to his readers the socialist "Great Emancipator" in such a light as to seek to make his socialism palatable to most Americans, as indeed it has become. (Benson, par. 4)

Benson goes on to add that

under the Lincoln Administration, we got the Internal Revenue Service, a strong national bank, federal funding for and promotion of education, and federal funding for "internal improvements" is hardly mentioned [by Sandburg]. Lincoln is mentioned as being a devoted disciple of Henry Clay, the father of "internal improvements." No one mentions the fact that Clay's "American System" of internal improvements was nothing more than socialism. (Benson, par. 5)

[…]

Carl Sandburg may or may not have had a political mind, but he had a most definite affinity for socialism and he sought to promote that, unconsciously or otherwise, in his work on Lincoln. (Benson, par.7)

The two-volume biography of Lincoln, although it sold enormously well, offended and perplexed many critics, in part because Sandburg undertook a difficult and unorthodox search for the "silent workings" of Lincoln's inner life (Niven 415). And as in all of his works published after 1922, Sandburg has both a specific and general social philosophy that sought to advance Socialist ideology, an ideology that was losing favor with most Americans in the 1920s. This is important to note because the juvenile biography titled *Abe Lincoln Grows Up* was taken from the first twenty-seven chapters of the original two-volume biography, and the imaginative construction of this work is well worth exploring.

The fact that Sandburg wrote both a biography of Lincoln suited for adult readers as well as a distilled version for younger readers is proof of his consistent and evolving iconoclastic and creative nature. As Al Benson explained above, Sandburg "had a most definite affinity for Socialism and he sought to promote that, unconsciously or otherwise, in his work on Lincoln" (Benson, par. 7). Sandburg knew that this biography could resituate Lincoln in the collective American imagination of adults. And a biography of Lincoln for young readers could do the same.

Like the biography for adults, the juvenile biography is a very complex work because it situates Lincoln within the context of American history, and, interestingly, it reveals many of Sandburg's sympathies. For example, throughout *Abe Lincoln Grows Up*, Sandburg explores how Native American Indians were often cheated out of their lands. In addition, Sandburg reveals both Lincoln's and his own deep and consistent sympathy for the slaves in this country. What young readers encounter in the opening lines of the first chapter immediately reveals Sandburg's sympathies:

> In the year 1776, when the thirteen colonies of England gave to the world that famous piece of paper known as the Declaration of Independence, there was a captain of Virginia militia living in Rockingham County, named Abraham Lincoln.
>
> He was a farmer with a 210-acre farm deeded to him by his father, John Lincoln, one of the many English, Scotch, Irish, German, Dutch settlers who were taking to the green hills and slopes of the Shenandoah Valley and putting their plows to ground never touched with farming tools by the red men, the Indians, who had held it for thousands of years. The work of driving out the red men so that the white men could farm in peace was not yet finished ... (4–5)

Passages like these reveal Sandburg's possible desire to implant in the minds of young readers the idea that white men victimized the "red men." At the time, this was a very unconventional way to present this segment of American history, and most Americans did not share his sympathies. Sandburg also complicates our view of the Lincoln family when he describes how

> Though they [the Lincolns] were fighting men, there was also a strain of Quaker blood running in them; they came in part from people who wore black clothes only, used the word "thee" instead of "you," kept silence or spoke "as the spirit of the heart moved," and held war to be a curse from hell; they were a serene, peaceable, obstinate people. (4–5)

One could argue that Sandburg offers characterizations like this in an attempt to help young readers understand a different dimension in the character that ran through the blood of the Lincoln family—a dimension of deep reverence, of thoughtfulness, and one that had a great antipathy for war. In essence, Sandburg was trying to rewrite history.

As the two-hundred-page juvenile biography moves forward, Sandburg's Socialist leanings become conspicuous. A representative passage appears very early in chapter one. Sandburg writes, "There had been papers signed, and the land belonged to the white men, but the red men couldn't understand or didn't wish to understand how the land was gone from them to the white men" (8). This passage shows residual vestiges of Sandburg's Socialist ideology, an ideology that permeates the first three volumes of poetry. In a 1919 letter to Romain Rolland, Sandburg articulates and clarifies his view of land and ownership:

> I believe all property is sacred for which men have wrestled with the wilderness or in any way toiled with their hands or brains or suffered and exchanged their lives and years to create ... In other words, the institution of property should be so ordained that no man should be granted owner-ship and title to property for which he has not rendered an equivalent, or nearly an equivalent, of service to society. Property is so sacred to me that I want to see it only in the hands of those who are able to take it and use it and make it of the greatest service to society. (qtd. in Mitgang 170)

These precepts fall in line with the political views articulated by Morris Hillquit in the mid-1910s, in his "Discussion and Testimony on Socialism and Trade Unionism Before the Commission on Industrial Relations." Hillquit, a member of the Socialist Party designated as the official representative of the Party, set forth the aims of his organization:

> ... under Socialism there would be no private ownership of industries, machinery, or any other means of exploiting a fellow man. There would be private ownership only in the means of consumption and enjoyment ... So long as there is no possibility for the exploitation of your fellow men by the ownership of the social tool—of the instrument of labor,—so far I do not see anything in the Socialist program that would prohibit the use and enjoyment of private property and its transmission to posterity. (Hillquit 85)

Much of Sandburg's work examines the issue of land ownership, especially *The People, Yes*. But Sandburg's biography of Lincoln not only examines the chasm between the rich and the poor but it also examines other social injustices. For example, the first chapter of *Abe Lincoln Grows Up* concludes with a statement that shows his interest in the nineteenth-century slavery issue in this country and makes clear Tom Lincoln's opposition. Sandburg writes:

> He [Tom Lincoln] had heard different preachers; some he liked better than others; some he was suspicious of; others he could listen to by the hour. There was a Reverend Jesse Head he had heard preach over at Springfield in Washington County, and he had a particular liking for Jesse Head, who was a good chair-maker, a good cabinet-maker, and an active exhorter in the branch of the Methodist church that stood against negro slavery and on that account had separated himself from the regular church. When

> Tom joined the Baptists it was in that branch of the church which was taking a stand against slavery. (13–4)

Abe Lincoln Grows Up, much like *Abraham Lincoln: The Prairie Years*, was critiqued for its fictional anecdotes and its many conjectures—all part of Sandburg's free use of imagination. For the record, it is true that Sandburg often speculated about conversations between family members. Admittedly, even though it is this element that often makes for a wonderful story, readers are forced to wonder if conversations like this one—describing the birth of Abraham Lincoln on February 12 of 1809—actually took place:

> And Dennis swung the baby back and forth, keeping up a chatter about how tickled he was to have a new cousin to play with. The baby screwed up the muscles of its face and began crying with no let-up.
>
> Dennis turned to Betsy Sparrow, handed her the baby and said to her, "Aunt, take him! He'll never amount to much."
>
> So came the birth of Abraham Lincoln that 12th of February in the year 1809—in silence and pain from a wilderness mother on a bed of corn-husks and bearskins—with an early laughing child prophecy he would never come to much. (34)

It is conversations, or "guesses" (Sherwood 1) like these that angered many Lincoln historians.

More examples of such passages can be seen throughout the narrative. For example, when Sandburg describes Nancy Hanks (the woman Tom Lincoln would eventually marry), he writes:

> She believed in God, in the Bible, in mankind, in the past and future, in babies, people, animals, flowers, fishes, in foundations and roofs, in time and the eternities outside of time; she was a believer, keeping in silence behind her gray eyes more beliefs than she spoke. She knew ... so much of what she believed was yonder. Every day came scrubbing, washing, patching, fixing. There was so little time to think or sing about the glory she believed in. It was always yonder. ... (26)

Carl Sandburg's *Abe Lincoln Grows Up* is a meticulously detailed, imaginative and stylistically vivid biography, and Sandburg's precision as a biographer must be noted. However, he had courage to take many creative liberties, whose ultimate purpose was to elevate Abraham Lincoln, the archetypal common man, to a mythical status—a status that would impress itself on the minds of young Americans all over the country. Passages like the following help to reveal this goal:

> ... though he was born in a house with only one door and one window, it was written he would come to know many doors, many windows; he would read many riddles and doors and windows. (34)

The biography is filled with passages that contribute to the idea of nation-building as well:

> The family lived there on Knob Creek farm, from the time Abe was three or so till he was past seven years of age. Here he was told "Kaintucky" meant the state he was living in; Knob Creek farm, the Rock Spring farm where he was born, Hodgenville, Elizabethtown, Muldraugh's Hill, these places he knew, the land he walked in, was all part of Kentucky.
>
> Yet it was also part of something bigger. Men had been fighting, bleeding, and dying in war, for a country, "our country"; a man couldn't have more than one country any more than he could have more than one mother; the name of the mother country was the "United States"; and there was a piece of cloth with red and white stripes having a blue square in its corner filled with white stars; and this piece of cloth they called "a flag." The flag meant the "United States." One summer morning his father started the day by stepping out of the front door and shooting a long rifle into the sky; and his father explained it was the day to make a big noise because it was the "Fourth of July," the day the United States first called itself a "free and independent" nation. (39–40)

Such passages make the biography distinctive and help to reveal what Carl Sandburg was attempting to do—resituate and re-present portions of American history to young readers in this country. Ultimately, Sandburg believed that all of his books—much like the movies Americans were watching all over the country—could directly serve as vehicles to re-tell American history.

In the juvenile biography, Sandburg not only discusses the spread of slavery in some parts of the country, but he addresses how other parts of the country witnessed a spread of freedom for Black men:

> Already, in parts of Kentucky and farther south, the poor white men, their women and children, were using the name of "nigger" for the slaves, while there were black slaves in families of quality who used the name of "po'w'ite" for the white people who owned only their clothes, furniture, a rifle, an ax, perhaps a horse and plow, and no land, no slaves, no stables, and no property to speak of.
>
> While these changes were coming in Kentucky, the territory of Indiana came into the Union as a state whose law declared "all men are born equally free and independent" and "the holding any part of the

human creation in slavery, or involuntary servitude, can only originate in usurpation and tyranny." In crossing the Ohio River's two shores, a traveler touched two soils, one where the buying and selling of black slaves went on, the other where the negro was held to be "part of human creation" and was not property for buying and selling. But both soils were part of the Union of the states. (56–7)

Passages like these force young readers to see the irrationality in the system of slavery. These passages also help young readers see how geographical zoning rendered something legal or illegal, moral or immoral.

In many other ways, Carl Sandburg's new imagination is manifested with great force and power throughout the juvenile Lincoln biography. One of the most representative passages appears in chapter ten:

And one night this boy [Abraham Lincoln] felt the southwest wind blowing the log-fire smoke into his nostrils. And there was a hoot-owl crying, and a shaking of branches in the beeches and walnuts outside, so that he went to the south opening of the shed and looked out on a winter sky with a high quarter-moon and a white shine of thin frost on the long open spaces of the sky.

And an old wonder took a deeper hold on him, a wonder about the loneliness of life down there in the Indiana wilderness, and a wonder about what was happening in other places over the world, places he had heard people mention, cities, rivers, flags, wars, Jerusalem, Washington, Baltimore.

He might have asked the moon, "What do you see?" And the moon might have told him many things.

That year of 1816 the moon had seen sixteen thousand wagons come along one turnpike in Pennsylvania, heading west, with people hungry for new land, a new home, just like Tom Lincoln. Up the Mississippi River that year had come the first steamboat to curve in to the Ohio River and land passengers at Louisville. The moon had seen the first steamboat leave Pittsburg and tie up at New Orleans. New wheels, wagons, were coming, an iron horse snorting fire and smoke. Rolling-mills, ingots, iron, steel, were the talk of Pennsylvania; a sheet copper mill was starting in Massachusetts.

The moon could see eight million people in the United States, white men who had pushed the Indians over the eastern mountains, fighting to clear the Great Plains and the southern valleys of the red men. At Fallen Timbers and at Tippecanoe in Indiana, and down at the Great Bend of the Tallapoosa, the pale faces and copper faces had yelled and grappled and Weatherford had said, "I have done the white people all the harm I could; if I had an army I would fight to the last; my warriors can no longer

> hear my voice; their bones are at Talladega, Tallushatches, Emuckfaw, and Tohopeka; I can do no more than weep." The red men had been warned by Jefferson to settle down and be farmers, to double their numbers every twenty years as the white people did, the whites in "new swarms continually advancing upon the country like flocks of pigeons."
>
> [...]
>
> And how these eight million people came to America, for the moon to look down on and watch their westward swarming? Many were children of men who had quarreled in the old countries of Europe, and fought wars about the words and ways of worshipping God and obeying His commandments. They were Puritans of England, French Huguenots, German Pietists, Hanoverians, Moravians, Saxons, Austrians, Swiss, Quakers, all carrying their Bibles ... (73–6)

Essentially, chapter ten is devoted to a semi-comprehensive retelling of world history. In addition to the quoted passages above, the chapter also alludes to the Lewis and Clark expedition, Napoleon "selling to Jefferson the Great Plains" (80), and "the pikes, roads, and trails heading west, broken wagon-wheels with prairie grass growing up over the spokes and hubs" (80).

This chapter, and many like it, highly imaginative in structure, giving the moon omniscience as well as a sagacious and impartial voice as it retells world history as it relates to American history, had its foreground in the creative imagination movies were fueling and shaping for Sandburg.

Additionally, chapter seventeen is entirely devoted to retelling, listing, and cataloging hundreds of superstitions as well as to cataloging hundreds of sayings. Again, like chapter ten, it is very unconventional in its style, and its only function seems to be to materialize Lincoln's countrymen. A representative example can be found early in the chapter when Sandburg writes:

> Potatoes, growing underground, must be planted in the dark of the moon, while beans, growing above ground, must be planted in the light of the moon. The posts of a rail fence would sink in the ground if not set in the dark of the moon. Trees for rails must be cut in the early part of the day and in the light of the moon. If in planting corn you skipped a row there would be a death in the family. If you killed the first snake you saw in the spring, you would win against all your enemies that year ... Feed gunpowder to dogs and it will make them fierce. To start on a journey and see a white mule is bad luck (124–25)

This interest in localized culture would eventually become a stylistic trademark for Sandburg. As a matter of fact, much of *Good Morning, America* (1928) and

The People, Yes (1936) reveal this same interest and style set in motion by the Lincoln biography. The opening poem of *Good Morning, America* is a case in point:

> A code arrives; language; lingo; slang;
> behold the proverbs of a people, a nation:
> Give 'em the works. Fix it, there's always
> a way. Be hard boiled. The good die young.
> [...]
> The big word is Service.
> Service—first, last and always.
> Business is business.
> What you don't know won't hurt you.
> Courtesy pays.
> Fair enough.
> The voice with a smile.
> Say it with flowers.
> Let one hand wash the other.
> The customer is always right ...
> There are lies, dam lies, and statistics.
> Figures don't lie but liars can figure.
> (*Complete Poems* 328–9)

Poem twenty-three in *The People, Yes* (1936) collects over thirty sayings, including,

> "A divorced man goes and marries the same kind of a woman he is just rid of," said the lawyer.
> "Don't mourn for me but organize," said the Utah I.W.W. before a firing squad executed sentence of death on him, his last words running: "Let her go!"
> "God will forgive me, it's his line of business," said the dying German-Jewish poet in his garret.
> (*Complete Poems* 463–4)

Once *Abe Lincoln Grows Up* enters the young adult phase of Lincoln's life, Sandburg devotes a laudatory chapter (chapter twenty-seven) to Andrew Jackson, concluding with a passage that might stand as a synopsis:

> He was well thought of by millions who believed there was truth lurking behind his sentiment, "True virtue cannot exist where pomp and parade are the governing passions; it can only dwell with the people—the great

> laboring and producing classes that form the bone and sinew of our
> confederacy." He was alluded to as "the Tennessee Barbarian" or "King
> Andrew the First" in certain circles, yet the doormats of the White House
> got acquainted with the shoes, boots, and moccasins of a wider range of
> humanity as he ran the Federal Government during those first years of the
> eight in which he was to be President." (186–87)

For Sandburg, Andrew Jackson embodied much of what he praised in Lincoln's character. He was a plain man and a plain people's hero, and this presentation of Lincoln within the shadow of Jackson, again, is essential to Sandburg's goal of nation-building. In the following passage, Sandburg explains how for Lincoln

> The personality and the ways of Andrew Jackson filled his thoughts. He
> asked himself many questions and puzzled his head about the magic of
> this one strong, stormy man filling the history of that year, commanding
> a wild love from many people, and calling out curses and disgust from
> others, but those others were very few in Indiana. The riddles that attach
> to a towering and magnetic personality staged before a great public, with
> no very definite issues or policies in question, but with some important
> theory of a government and art of life apparently involved behind the
> personality—these met young Abe's eyes and ears. (188–9)

Sandburg continues to carefully articulate the forces influencing and shaping Lincoln's sense of self as well as his worldview. For example, at the conclusion of chapter twenty-eight, Sandburg explains how

> Young nineteen-year-old Abe Lincoln had plenty to think about in that
> year of 1828, what with his long trip to New Orleans and back, what
> with the strong, stormy Andrew Jackson sweeping into control of the
> Government at Washington, and the gentle, teasing, thoughtful words of
> Thomas Jefferson: "Sometimes it is said that man cannot be trusted with
> the government of himself. Can he then be trusted with the government
> of others?" (190)

Immediately following the chapter describing Andrew Jackson appears a celebratory chapter describing the lives of Johnny Appleseed and John James Audubon. Sandburg explains how Johnny Appleseed "had been making his name one to laugh at and love in the log cabins between the Ohio River and the northern lakes" (191). Sandburg presents Johnny Appleseed as a "primitive Christian" (195), a common man. He quotes John James Audubon, who after reading a paper before the Natural History Society of London on the habits of the wild pigeon, wrote:

> Captain Hall expressed some doubts as to my views respecting the affection and love of pigeons, as if I made it [sic] human, and raised the possessors quite above the brutes. I presume the love of the (pigeon) mothers for their young is much the same as the love of woman for her offspring. There is but one kind of love: God is love, and all his creatures derive theirs from his; only it is modified by the different degrees of intelligence in different beings and creatures. (198)

Sandburg clearly wanted to fuse the images of Jackson, Appleseed, and Audubon into a composite and overlay that onto our understanding of Lincoln. In essence, these three men provided a prism—one by which we readers could come to understand Lincoln more accurately.

Abe Lincoln Grows Up follows Lincoln's life from birth in 1809 to age twenty-two in 1831. The final chapter of the book ends with Lincoln again floating down the Mississippi River, this time working for Denton Offut, a man who had hired him, John Hanks, and John Johnston to "go onto Government timber-land and get out gunwales for the flatboat, while the rest of the needed lumber could come from Kirkpatrick's sawmill, charged to Offut" (216).

The final chapter also discusses how, once in New Orleans, Lincoln confronted the issue of slavery point-blank. He saw the advertisements and heard the trader's notices. He even saw "one auction in New Orleans where an octoroon girl was sold, after being pinched, trotted up and down, and handled so the buyer could be satisfied she was sound of wind and limb" (221).

The biography ends with Lincoln back in Illinois, saying "good-by to home and the family roof" (221) before "going out into the big world to make a place for himself" (222).

Chapter 7

A New Type of American Biography: Resituating Lincoln's Place in American History—Abraham Lincoln: The Prairie Years

I n a somewhat hostile 1925 letter to Albert J. Beveridge, a statesman who was writing what would eventually become one of the major biographies of Lincoln, Sandburg explained how his own biography of Lincoln would distinguish itself from others:

> The issue that you have raised, in private conversations, implies your beliefs that your writings are to be "authentic" and mine not. This may run back to a personal habit of yours of speaking freely or loosely, in private conversations, or it may involve an antagonism as to method, a chasm in points of view as to presentation of materials. In either case I have the advantage of you that exists between two men where one has the familiar facts that enable him to understand and measure the elements of sincerity in the case. It would be gratuitous to point out that your own character will get written into your Lincoln work, in degree, as inevitably as it did in your [biography of] Marshall. (qtd. in Mitgang 233 [italics in original])

This distinction delineated by Sandburg reveals great self-confidence in his work and stresses his knowledge and intimacy with "the familiar facts" of Lincoln's life, a characteristic that serves as the cornerstone of his 1926 Lincoln biography—*Abraham Lincoln: The Prairie Years*.

This sense of intimacy with "the familiar facts" came from his diligent collection of information on Lincoln, which started in the early 1900s (Callahan, *Carl Sandburg* 121). Also, since that time Sandburg had used his extensive travels not only to make a living, but to help him collect Lincoln material, "'listening to old men's reminiscences, walking the paths that Lincoln walked,' communicating with Lincoln collectors, and scouring secondhand bookstores and purchasing books" (Callahan 122). This is precisely what Sandburg had in mind when he told Beveridge that he "had the advantage ... where one has the familiar facts that enable him to understand and measure the elements of sincerity in the case" (qtd. in Mitgang 233).

Karl Detzer, author of *Carl Sandburg: A Study in Personality and Background* (1941), offers a key insight into Carl Sandburg's two separately published biographies of Lincoln—*Abraham Lincoln: The Prairie Years* (1926) and *Abraham Lincoln: The War Years* (1939). Detzer confirms the intimacy of the Lincoln portrait Sandburg wanted to offer when he explains how "Sandburg was inside Lincoln looking out through Lincoln's eyes, seeing the world as Lincoln saw it, saying the things he would have said" (166). North Callahan explains it quite similarly when he says:

> What Carl Sandburg was undertaking can be compared to a journalistic assignment in which a reporter is asked to do, instead of a straight, factual account, a feature story. The feature writer relates the same story but embellishes it with colorful touches, additional decorations, and even imaginative flourishes. Carl Sandburg wrote a feature story about Abraham Lincoln. (Callahan, *Carl Sandburg* 122–23)

In his biography of Carl Sandburg, Callahan goes on to clarify how, as was the case for many Americans, Abraham Lincoln was a figure of tremendous interest for Sandburg since boyhood. Callahan also confirms that while Sandburg was in his early twenties, he read "all of the Ida Tarbell articles on Lincoln in *McClure's Magazine*, followed by Herndon's life of Lincoln, and then the Nicolay and Hay life of Lincoln as serialized in *Century Magazine*" (Callahan 121). But there were many other very important biographies of Lincoln that were very different, and that preceded Sandburg's biography of Lincoln.

To establish and advance "the Lincoln legend," the William H. Herndon and Jesse W. Weik three-volume biography, titled *Herndon's Life of Lincoln*, had been published in 1889. The John G. Nicolay and John Hay ten-volume biography of Lincoln, titled *Abraham Lincoln: A History*, appeared the following year in 1890. Not only were these some of the earliest and most comprehensive biographies written on Lincoln, but they helped to set in motion "the Lincoln legend." As Carl Van Doren's *The Literary Works of Abraham Lincoln* (1942) brilliantly points out, "The Lincoln legend is one of America's magnificent achievements. The man he was has long been made over into the hero he will continue to be today" (Van Doren xvi).

There is little doubt that Carl Sandburg's two separately published Lincoln biographies fueled renewed interest in the figure of Lincoln and in the Civil War era. Equally important, Sandburg's biographies of Lincoln were not only radically different from those that preceded them, but they served as the introductory centerpieces in his literary project of nation-building.

Examining how these two separate biographies of Lincoln incorporate a new imagination and contribute to his project of nation-building will be the focus of this chapter. To better frame the chapter, though, it is essential to quote from Malcolm Bradbury's useful essay "The American Risorgimento: The United States and the Coming of the New Arts":

> The cosmopolitan and national construction of the modern American tradition in fiction and poetry over the first two decades of the century, which is my theme here, was to reach its greatest point of enrichment during the 1920s. Inescapably related to the extraordinary transformation of the arts that passed through the Western nations from the 1890s to the period of reassessment that followed the First World War, it acquired, by selective assimilation and emendation by American myths and American versions of tradition, its own flavours. These had to do with a different experience of history, a different attitude toward myth, a different view of the prospect of the future; they had also to do with that endeavour to recover a usable American past which would allow the American arts to break free of European dependencies. (qtd. in Cunliffe 25–6)

Indeed, Carl Sandburg used his Lincoln biographies to offer American audiences "a different experience of history, a different attitude toward myth, a different view of the prospect of the future." In addition, he wanted to "recover a usable American past"—a goal whose aim was to have America look to itself for models in this era of growth and change.

Ultimately, for Sandburg, Lincoln was the archetypal common man because of his honesty, simplicity, and spiritual depth and growth. Additionally, Sandburg's portrait of Lincoln is that of a man who saw the political and the personal as intertwined. This imaginative characterization of Lincoln would be presented to a post-war America that was radically different from the America in which Abraham Lincoln had lived. The America of the 1920s saw "change and development, as technological and material advance speeded, lifestyle changed and experimentalism in art complemented a sense of historical experimentalism in life" (qtd. in Cunliffe 26).

Harry Golden's *Carl Sandburg* (1961) offers a salient insight into Sanburg's effort to recover a usable American past:

> Sandburg was the first American poet able to use and exploit slang in his diction. He was the first poet to incorporate concrete political and social images into his poems; both radical innovations.

His most noted works, *The Prairie Years* and *The War Years*, the biography of Lincoln, were also radical. For the truth is that with the exception of Lincoln's own writings, the Civil War did not produce a great literature. It was not until Stephen Crane published *The Red Badge of Courage*, Stephen Vincent Benét his *John Brown's Body*, and Sandburg his six volumes totaling over a million words on Lincoln that a substantial literature about the Civil War existed. That Sandburg made literature from the Civil War is also a radical vision. (Golden 116)

Readers need to remember that since 1865, the figure of Abraham Lincoln had been firmly etched in the national psyche, and although Lincoln was never forgotten, Sandburg wanted to present a new kind of imaginative portrait of Lincoln told in a narrative form that only he could write. Although Sandburg was well acquainted with what previous Lincoln biographers had said about his life and his presidency, Sandburg wanted to tell Lincoln's story in his own way. Sandburg knew what Lincoln once meant to the country and was hopeful of what he could once again come to mean to average Americans in the twentieth century. Unlike previously published biographies of Lincoln—primarily aimed at academicians and historians—his biography would be aimed at the common people of this country, and this intention, too, reveals Sandburg's dramatic artistic experimentation.

Lincoln, of course, had been deified almost immediately after his death. According to the reactionary Greg Loren Durand, author of *America's Caesar: The Decline and Fall of Republican Government in the United States of America* (2005), the

Cult of Lincoln was founded on 15 April 1865 when a single bullet altered what otherwise would have been his rightful place alongside history's bloodiest rulers. Up until the time of his death, Lincoln was denounced by nearly everyone in Washington, including the men of his own party and the members of his own Cabinet as "a more unlimited despot that the world knows this side of China," "a despicable tyrant," "that original gorilla," and "a low, cunning clown." (Durand, par. 2)

Durand goes on to argue that "These denunciations ceased with Lincoln's last breath, when the real Lincoln suddenly vanished from public record to be replaced by a figure resembling the mythical gods of Pagan Rome more than a man" (Durand, par. 5).

Biographical treatments of Lincoln, the first of which appeared the year after his death abetted the apotheosis of Lincoln. Two themes emerged in Lincoln biographies following his death. One took its cue from the eulogies and emphasized Lincoln's high principles and saintliness; the other stressed his backwoods western origins. Josiah G. Holland's depiction of Lincoln as a martyr-saint endowed with all the Christian virtues, contained in his 1866 (the year following Lincoln's death) *Life of Abraham Lincoln,* proved immensely popular; the book sold more than 100,000 copies. In Holland's view, Lincoln was a model youth who rose on the strength of his merit and high ideals. Holland characterized Lincoln as "savior of the republic, emancipator of a race, true Christian, true man." The portrayal of Lincoln as a combination of Christ and George Washington was echoed in dozens of other nineteenth-century biographies. ("Chapter Two," par. 5)

Roy Basler's *The Lincoln Legend: A Study in Changing Conceptions* (1935) also brilliantly explains how

The controversies surrounding Lincoln's conduct of the war and the virulent personal attacks on him were forgotten, and Americans celebrated his idealism, fairness, compassion, devotion to duty, and vision of the future. Lincoln was compared to George Washington and praised as the second savior of the republic. Clergymen and others stressed Lincoln's Christ-like attributes; details of Lincoln's life—an obscure birth, a carpenter father, and assassination on Good Friday inevitably reinforced the connection. (3)

Walt Whitman's 1865 poem "When Lilacs Last in the Dooryard Bloom'd" lauded Lincoln as "the sweetest, wisest soul of all my days and lands" and portrayed him as "the grandest figure on the crowded canvas of the drama of the nineteenth century" ("Chapter Two," par. 4). But Whitman was only one of hundreds of poets who dedicated verse tributes to Lincoln. Herman Melville, Julia Ward Howe, William Cullen Bryant, James Russell Lowell, and Oliver Wendell Holmes also wrote memorial poems. An entire volume of *Poetical Tributes* (1865) included the works of poets from all the northern states, seven southern states, and three foreign countries. Letters of the period routinely referred to Lincoln as "The Great Emancipator" or the "Great Martyr" (Basler 168).

Carl Sandburg thought it essential to build on this mythical characterization of Lincoln. His long labors yielded *Abraham Lincoln: The Prairie Years* in 1926 and *Abraham Lincoln: The War Years* in 1939. But it must be stressed again that Sandburg's two biographies of Lincoln—totaling over one million words and twenty years of painstaking toil and labor—were significantly different from any of the previously published biographies. What made the biographies strange and unique rested on his use of a new imagination, one that allowed him to tell Lincoln's story very differently than it had ever been told. As Richard Crowder states, "Sandburg followed the man every step of the way; and wherever the next step was shadowy he speculated, sometimes in a kind of free-verse fantasy" (Crowder 95). This new imagination—a poetic license of a new kind—was being practiced in a genre that traditionally requires the strictest adherence to fact. As both biographer and historian, Sandburg meticulously presents precise chronological facts as well as poignant insights about Lincoln's character, and he also flawlessly contextualizes Lincoln's life within the landscape of American history.

Presenting Lincoln as a common man "whose memory was cross-indexed with tangled human causes" (*The Prairie Years and The War Years* [One vol. ed.] 128), Sandburg's understanding of Lincoln was penetrating, personal, and perhaps timeless. Indeed, Sandburg not only wanted to tell readers about Lincoln's life, he also wanted to offer them "a different experience of history, a different attitude toward myth, a different view of the prospect of the future" (qtd. in Cunliffe 25–6). Sandburg was on a mission to create a profile of Lincoln as the archetypal common man.

In the "Preface" to the 1926 biography of *Abraham Lincoln: The Prairie Years*, Sandburg articulates the difficulty of capturing the "outline and lights and shadows and changing tints to call out portraits of him in his Illinois backgrounds and settings—even had he never been elected President" (vii). He then immediately turns his attention to providing an exhaustive time line that informs readers about the many biographies written of Lincoln, and, additionally, makes an effort to mention the hundreds of sources that he consulted in preparation for the book. This five-page section of the "Preface" is very scholarly in tone and couches the biography in scholarly terms. Sandburg even notes his use of the "bibliography of Daniel Fish, published in 1906, [which] listed 1,080 books," adding that "J. B. Oakleaf of Moline, Illinois, bringing the Fish enumeration to the year 1925, adds 1,600 items" (ix). He also identifies all of the major Lincoln collections across the country that he consulted and cites many articles from local newspapers that "supplied quaint original material" (x).

The biography at times reads like a book written with the care and the precision of a trained historian and biographer, but in other instances it radically transforms itself into what seems to be a loving tribute and poetic epic, making Lincoln its larger-than-life hero. Though the acknowledgment section included at the end of the biography lists hundreds of books that were central to Sandburg's writing, throughout the narrative itself no footnotes or endnotes are to be found. Interestingly, Sandburg makes an effort to quote heavily from personal letters and primary sources he had collected, but never does he cite specific sources. The text, then, is never over-burdened or weighed down—giving it a different feel from more "scholarly" Lincoln biographies, one more suited to the average American reader.

For many historians, it was this very characteristic that made the work frustrating to read. Mark Neely explains how Sandburg "accumulated masses of fascinating details, but never felt it necessary to organize them, to impose systematic historical understanding on them, or even to sort out the important from the trivial" (Neely 381).

Not surprisingly—as had been the case with *Slabs of the Sunburnt West* (1922), *Rootabaga Stories* (1922), and *Rootabaga Pigeons* (1923)—American readers warmly received this biography. Not only did Sandburg broaden the audience for books on Lincoln, but as Henry Steele Commanger noted in the 1940 issue of *The Yale Review*, his secret was that he "realized that Lincoln belongs to the people, not to the historians" (qtd. in Salwak 53).

Ronald Mace, who has written several short critical pieces on Sandburg's Lincoln biography explains how

> Sandburg employs his poetic imagination to recreate many scenes that he feels, by all rights, should and must have taken place. While there is no evidence to support the accuracy of Sandburg's guesses, and in spite of the fact that he often weaves the fact and the fanciful together without distinction, the entire work rings true to the spirit of the Lincoln we come to see later on.
>
> Sandburg has said that he had wanted to take Lincoln out of the hands of the sentimentalists and false politicians who made him into a supporter of the most absurd and contradictory political ideas. He wanted to give the reader a true portrait of the man as he saw him, and this meant partly as a man and partly as a mythical figure of the Midwestern prairie. The biography, in fact, succeeds in accomplishing this goal. (9)

Mace goes on to offer an additional incisive insight worth repeating:

> In summing up the entire achievement of the six volumes, Golden asks the critical question, "Who doubts that in his *Lincoln* biography Carl Sandburg was trying to articulate the American myth?" There is then a sense in which Sandburg's Lincoln is a mythical figure in addition to being a factual person. He is a representative of "what America could and morally ought to be," as well as what it actually was. The myth, though, is derived not out of any sentimentalizing emotionalism, but out of a deep

> understanding of the meaning of Lincoln in the life of America. Golden
> shows that this aim was intentional on the part of Sandburg. He quotes
> from *A Lincoln Preface* which Sandburg published in a limited edition for
> his personal friends shortly before the appearance of *The War Years*, and
> which is not available to the general public. It is obvious that Sandburg felt
> that Lincoln has a major place in history and that he is the representative
> figure of an entire nation as were the men to whom he is compared.
> (Mace 84 [italics in original])

The two biographies, in essence then, showing Lincoln in all of his complexity, embody the collective spirit of the people in this country.

Much of the project of nation-building took on the form of trying to capture and articulate Lincoln's ideology concerning his optimism in the belief and goal of achieving basic equality for all Americans. One such passage appears early in the biography, in a section describing Lincoln's first attempt at "stepping into politics as a candidate for the legislature of the state of Illinois" (27) in 1832. In a handbill printed by the *Sangamo Journal* in Springfield, Lincoln was quoted as saying:

> That every man may receive at least, a moderate education, and thereby
> be enabled to read the histories of his own and other countries, by which
> he may duly appreciate the value of our free institutions, appears to be an
> object of vital importance, even on this account alone, to say nothing of
> the advantages and satisfaction to be derived from all being able to read
> the scriptures and other works, both of a religious and moral nature, for
> themselves. (27)

Sandburg then proceeds to explain how Lincoln denounced "the practice of loaning money at exorbitant rates of interest," and supported creating a law setting a limit to the rates of usury (27). Here, we see Lincoln's belief that the many should not suffer at the hands of the few. (It is interesting that Lincoln, although never a conventionally religious man, saw education as a vehicle for receiving "the advantages and satisfaction to be derived from all being able to read the scriptures and other works, both of a religious and moral nature, for themselves.") These two passages are very characteristic of Sandburg's work—the first reveals the optimism the young Lincoln had in himself as well as the promise and potential he saw in the American people; the second reveals Lincoln's criticisms of many of the most serious social problems plaguing American society. Similar instances appear in the Lincoln books repeatedly. In essence, they typify Sandburg's aim to present Lincoln as a man who was more than one-dimensional; instead, he was a man with ideals and vision, firmly grounded in the events of his time.

Worth underscoring and absolutely central to this discussion also is the idea that Carl Sandburg's biography of Abraham Lincoln—and a foundation for his project of nation-building—centers on the characterization of Lincoln as a man of the people. Virtually every action Lincoln took, even from a young age, had the ultimate aim of improving the lives of his countrymen. There was nothing selfish or self-serving about Abraham Lincoln, and this factor becomes the lynchpin of Sandburg's project of nation-building.

One of the most often quoted passages among Lincoln scholars, including Sandburg, embodies this particular altruism seemingly innate to his character. When asked early in his political career what his ambition was, Lincoln offered the following response:

> I have no other so great as that of being truly esteemed of my fellow men, by rendering my self worthy of their esteem. ... I was born and have ever remained in the most humble walks of life. I have no wealthy or popular relations to recommend me. ... If the good people in their wisdom shall see fit to keep me in the background, I have been too familiar with disappointments to be very much chagrined. (28)

This desire to "being truly esteemed [by his] fellow man" is what Sandburg wanted readers to understand about Lincoln's character, because this is Sandburg's strategy to resituate how Americans saw Lincoln, and, in turn, how they saw themselves within the context of their changing country.

In *Abraham Lincoln: The Prairie Years*, Sandburg carefully traces Lincoln's every step, from birth to his ascension to the White House. Sandburg's Lincoln is a mere mortal, shaped by the attitudes of his time and place. As a result, Sandburg's readers learn about Lincoln's 1832 enlistment in a company of Independent Rangers in their battle against Black Hawk. His direct involvement in this battle allowed Lincoln to get a first-hand view of war, and through this experience, Sandburg clarifies how "In those days Lincoln had seen deep into the heart of the American volunteer soldier, why men go to war, march in mud, sleep in rain on cold ground, eat pork raw when it can't be boiled, and kill when the killing is good. On a later day an observer was to say he saw Lincoln's eyes misty in his mention of the American volunteer soldier" (32). Sandburg's Abraham Lincoln is a mere mortal who grew up close to the land and the people, and he recognized the problems facing the several local communities he lived in throughout his life as well as the problems facing the nation.

Sandburg's portrait of Lincoln also captures the sagacity, the unshakable moral core, and the irreverent wit Lincoln possessed, characteristics and dimensions of his personality that many previously published Lincoln biographies may never have captured quite as dramatically. A representative passage that illustrates Sandburg's insightful characterization of Lincoln appears in a chapter titled "The Young Legislator." Sandburg describes a clash Lincoln had with a young Springfield lawyer named George Forquer, "who had switched from Whig to Democrat, then being appointed by the Jackson administration as register of the land office at $3,000 a year. On his elegant new frame house Forquer had put up the first lightning rod in that part of Illinois, a sight people went out of their way to see" (49).

During a speech Lincoln delivered in the courthouse in Sangamon County, he responded to a criticism Forquer had aimed at him. Lincoln is quoted as saying, "I desire to live, and I desire place and distinction; but I would rather die now than, like the gentleman, live to see the day that I would change my politics for an office worth three thousand dollars a year, and then feel compelled to erect a lightning rod to protect a guilty conscience from an offended God" (49). This very real portrait of Lincoln in all his complexity and irreverent wit is what Sandburg aimed to offer his readers. Ultimately, Sandburg's Lincoln is a real man who did the best he could with the faculties he had been given. Sandburg knew that if he hoped to immerse the common reader in a comprehensive lesson in American history, he would have to present to them a man who was one of them. In this same chapter, Sandburg explains how

> In the Southern states it was against the law to speak against slavery; agitators of slave revolts would be hanged and had been. The 3,000,000 Negro workers in the Southern States on the tax books were livestock valued at more than a billion dollars. In political parties and churches, in business partnerships and families, the slavery question was beginning to split the country in two. (53)

Surprisingly, Sandburg's Lincoln, serving in the state legislature of Illinois at the time, recorded this mixed protest regarding slavery:

> Resolutions upon the subject of domestic slavery having passed both branches of the General Assembly at its present session, the undersigned hereby protest against the passage of the same.
>
> They believe that the institution of slavery is founded on both injustice and bad policy; but that the promulgation of abolition doctrines tends rather to increase than abate its evils.

> They believe that the Congress of the United States has no power
> under the constitution, to interfere with the institution of slavery in the
> different States. (53)

This statement articulates Lincoln's early position on the slavery problem. It is shocking to hear these somewhat counterintuitive words coming from "the Great Emancipator," because here Lincoln is at once criticizing slavery and conceding the point that "Congress ... has no power under the Constitution, to interfere with the institution of slavery in the different States." But, again, it was Sandburg's aim to give readers a fully complex portrait of the man Lincoln was.

In this same chapter, Sandburg notes that Lincoln early on engaged in "sarcasm and satire that was to bring him shame and humiliation. He would change. He was to learn, at cost, how to use the qualities of pity and compassion that lay deeply and naturally in his heart, toward wiser reading and keener understanding of all men and women he met" (60).

Throughout the biography, Sandburg takes broader historical events and connects them specifically to the life of Lincoln. In a speech delivered to the Young Men's Lyceum of Springfield in January of 1838, Lincoln gave an address titled "The Perpetuation of Our Political Institutions," in which he responds to events like the riot that left the abolitionist Elijah Parish Lovejoy dead. Sandburg noted that Lincoln's theme in the speech was "the spirit of violence in men overriding law and legal procedure" (64). Lincoln said, "… whenever the vicious portion of population shall be permitted to gather … and burn churches, ravage and rob provision stores, throw printing presses into rivers, shoot editors, and hang and burn obnoxious persons at pleasure, and with impunity; depend on it, this Government cannot last" (64). Sandburg explains how in this speech Lincoln "dealt with the momentous sacred ideas, basic in love of the American Dream, of personal liberty and individual responsibility. They were seeds in his mind foreshadowing growth. He spoke a toleration of free discussion. …" (64).

The central idea here is that Lincoln "dealt with the momentous sacred ideas." Ultimately, it is Lincoln's unique ability to recognize what is important about his local community and view these problems within a national framework as well as within a historical and universal context that Sandburg wants to stress. A few pages later Lincoln tells his best friend Joshua Speed how "he wished to live to connect his name with events of his day and generation and to the interest of his fellow men" (70). Again, this is the imaginative characterization of Lincoln that Sandburg was aiming to create—one of a man who felt deeply entwined in the ebb and flow of the events shaping America.

As is the case with *Rootabaga Stories* and *Rootabaga Pigeons*, scores of passages throughout the biography seem to echo major tenets of Socialist ideology. Although Carl Sandburg's devotion to the Socialist Party had dissipated by 1919, his interests in the ideals of the Socialist Party had not. (We should remember that between 1900 and 1914 Sandburg supported the Socialist Party and wrote hundreds of articles, essays, and poems for many Socialist newspapers and magazines). As a result, many residual Socialist elements appear in the Lincoln biography. This is important in Sandburg's project of nation-building because in Sandburg's view, Lincoln was the ideal Socialist.

A good example of this imaginative characterization of Lincoln can be seen when Sandburg recounts how Lincoln often in his very personal writing revealed his independent thinking. These private thoughts give us deeper insight into Lincoln's mind and soul, but the passages Sandburg selects to include resound with the tenets of Socialism:

> In the early days of the world, the Almighty said to the first of our race "In the sweat of thy face shalt thou eat bread"; and since then, if we except the light and the air of heaven, no good thing has been, or can be enjoyed by us, without having first cost labour. And, inasmuch [as] most good things are produced by labour, it follows that [all] such things of right belong to those whose labour has produced them. But it has so happened in all ages of the world, that some have laboured, and others have, without labour, enjoyed a large proportion of the fruits. This is wrong and should not continue ... (88)

This passage parallels Sandburg's understanding of Socialist tenets, as expounded in the letter to Romain Rolland in 1919, "... I repeat that all property created by man's labor is sacred to me and such property should be protected, invested with safeguards and a machinery of production and distribution wherethrough the man who works would receive the product of his work ..." (qtd. in Mitgang 170).

Another passage in the biography that reverberates with Socialist ideals appears several chapters later when Sandburg describes the emerging social classes in society. He writes, "The transcontinental railroad, the iron-built, ocean-going steamship, the power-driven factory—the owners and managers of these are to be a new breed of rulers of the earth" (114). This passage describes the chasm in the class structure in America—a class structure that was very pronounced in the late nineteenth and early twentieth centuries.

And there are other passages in the biography that present a deeper and more politically radical Lincoln. Early in chapter seven, within the context of

Mexico gaining independence from Spain and Texas, Sandburg relates Lincoln's views on the people's right to revolution. Lincoln writes:

> Any people anywhere, being inclined and having the power, have the right to rise up, and shake off the existing government, and form a new one that suits them better. ... Any portion of such people that can, may revolutionize, and make their own, of so much the territory as they inhabit. More than this, a majority of any portion of such people may revolutionize, putting down a minority, intermingled with, or near about them, who may oppose their movement. Such minority, was precisely the case, of the tories of our own revolution. It is a quality of revolutions not to go by old lines, or old laws; but to break up both, and make new ones. (95)

This passage reveals Lincoln's clear understanding of the nature of revolution, and it also reveals the inherent power he believes "the People" possess. Lincoln recognizes that common men and women are the ones that fight the battles and shed the blood, and Lincoln's reverence for their collective power helps illuminate the mind of the man that would eventually ascend to the office of the presidency. This characterization of Lincoln's view helps to advance Sandburg's project of nation-building—a project that aimed to further empower Americans living in the 1920s.

By 1858, Lincoln's sense of self is deep, and his political ideas are well shaped and fully thought out. A good example can be seen in a meditation he wrote that year concerning his position on slavery:

> ... Yet I have never failed—do not now fail—to remember that in the republican cause there is a higher aim than that of mere office. I have not allowed myself to forget that the abolition of the Slave-trade by Great Brittain [sic] was agitated a hundred years before it was a final success; that the measure had it's [sic] open fire-eating opponents; it's [sic] dollar and cent opponents; it's [sic] inferior race opponents; its negro equality opponents; and its religion and good order opponents; that all these opponents got offices, and their adversaries got none. But I have also remembered that though they blazed, like tallow-candles for a century, at last they flickered in the socket, died out, stank in the dark for a brief season, and were remembered no more, even by the smell ... I am proud, in my passing speck of time, to contribute an humble mite to that glorious consummation, which my own poor eyes may not last to see. (Sandburg, *Abraham Lincoln* [*Reader's Digest ed.*] 136)

Lincoln possessed all of the necessary insights of mind, soul, and character to help guide him during his first and second terms as president. Sandburg's aim with the biography was, in part, to get readers to see Lincoln in all of his complexity and to get them to develop their own insights of mind, soul, and character.

On November 6, 1860, with exactly 1,866,452 votes, Abraham Lincoln, soon to be fifty-two years old, defeated Stephen A. Douglas (1,376,957 votes) and John Breckenridge (849,781). The electoral count reveals how soundly Lincoln won: Lincoln, 180; Breckenridge, 72, and Douglas, 12 (Boyer xxvi). Within a month of the election, fearful and disgusted by Lincoln's victory, South Carolina, Georgia, Alabama, Mississippi, Florida, Louisiana, and Texas left the Union. Lincoln's initial position on the secession of the South is described by Sandburg when he writes, "He [Lincoln] argued that seceded states had no right to secede, yet the Federal Government had no right to use force to stop them from seceding. He urged, however, the right of the Federal Government to use force against individuals, in spite of secession, to enforce Federal laws and hold Federal property" (Sandburg, *Abraham Lincoln* [*Reader's Digest ed.*] 166).

Chapter 8

The Archetypal Common Man—Abraham Lincoln:
The War Years

T he opening pages of Sandburg's four-volume, million-word plus Pulitzer Prize-winning *Abraham Lincoln: The War Years* (published thirteen years after *Abraham Lincoln: The Prairie Years*) documents the journey of the American republic from the time Lincoln took office to the years immediately after his death in 1865. The opening paragraphs of the first chapter (titled "America—Whither?") carefully frame the years Lincoln was to serve in office:

> The famous lawyer, Rufus Choate, listening to foreign-language grand opera in New York, had told his daughter to be sure to let him know when to laugh or cry or just sit still and keep cool. From the shifting stage scenes he could hear words, but he didn't know what they were saying. He needed help. "Interpret for me the libretto lest I dilate with wrong emotion," he told the daughter.
>
> Men and women in this mood in early 1861 looked on the American scene and listened and wished they could tell what the noise and pain meant today and was going to mean next week. (*The War Years* 3)

Sandburg, here, captures the anticipated political, social, and cultural tumult that would run parallel to Lincoln's presidency.

Unlike *Abraham Lincoln: The Prairie Years*, this new biography "had no single theme and appeared to most reviewers to give almost a journalistic chronicle of the developing Lincoln administration" (Neely 379). Upon its publication,

> *The War Years* was widely acclaimed as a literary masterpiece, though it was less markedly literary than *The Prairie Years*. Professional historians, customarily grudging in their praise of amateurs, also commended the books. James G. Randall, soon to be the dean of scholarly Lincoln biographers, said in 1942 that Sandburg's made all other Lincoln books "dull or stupid by comparison." He and Sandburg became friends, and Randall

gained a reputation in later years as one of the few academic defenders of Sandburg's work. (Neely 380)

The portrait Sandburg offered of Lincoln was one of a stern war chief who had unshifting convictions. As in the previous biography, Lincoln was presented as a very real man, full of depth, complexities, and contradictions—and one always connected to the needs of "the People." And, again, as was the case in *Abraham Lincoln: The Prairie Years*, Lincoln is the representative figure of an entire nation.

Sandburg also knew that in the 1930s America needed a figure like Abraham Lincoln—for the figure of Lincoln embodied optimism and represented the potential for a genuine and working democracy. In these years of the Great Depression, Sandburg published *The People, Yes* (1936) and *Abraham Lincoln: The War Years* (1939). He hoped Lincoln would remind the people of this country, as well as their elected leaders, that America was a land of Democracy and a land where the government and "the People" worked together. Stephen Vincent Benét was one of the first critics to offer a review of the Lincoln biography in December of 1939 in *The Atlantic Monthly*:

> ... this is a biography, not only of Abraham Lincoln, but of the Civil War. The great, the near-great, the wretched, the commonplace, the humble, the shoddy—dozens, hundreds of men and women, known or little known, who played their part in those years—generals, civilians, office seekers, Congressmen, cranks, soldiers of the North and South, traitors, spies, plain citizens—appear and disappear like straws whirled along by a torrent.
> [...]
> ... I think it is difficult for anyone to read these volumes and not come out, at the end, with a renewed faith in the democracy that Lincoln believed in and a renewed belief in the America he sought. They are a good purge for our own troubled time and for its more wild-eyed fears. (Marowski 348)

Benét correctly underscores Sandburg's primary intention for the biography—to give Americans "a renewed faith in the democracy that Lincoln believed in and a renewed belief in the America he sought."

From the first moment of his presidency, Lincoln's personal and political actions are aimed at preserving the Union, giving freedom and equality to all, and trusting the collective voice of the common people of this country. A good example is articulated in a speech that Lincoln delivered on February 22, 1861—the day that Kansas was admitted to the union. Lincoln says, "The man does not live who is more devoted to peace than I am. None who would do more to preserve it. But it may be necessary to put the foot down firmly. And if I do my duty, and do right, you will sustain me, will you not?" (178). He later adds that with his honest heart, he "dares not tell that I bring a head sufficient for it" (180), but he would lean on the people: "If my own strength should fail, I shall at least fall back upon these masses, who, I think, under any circumstances will not fail" (Sandburg, *Abraham Lincoln: The Prairie Years and the War Years* [*Reader's Digest ed.*] 180).

Throughout his presidency, there is an echo of the words he shared with the country during his First Inaugural Address. Sandburg underscores Lincoln's unwavering allegiance to the Union, the Constitution, and to the common people who elected him to office—who provide the backbone of this country—and who live close to the bone and marrow of life. On March 4, 1861, in his Inaugural Address, Lincoln told his countrymen that

> ... I shall take care, as the Constitution itself expressly enjoins me, that the laws of the Union be faithfully executed in all the States. Doing this I deem to be only a simple duty on my part; and I shall perform it, so far as practicable, unless my rightful masters, the American people, shall withhold the requisite means, or, in some authoritative manner, direct the contrary.
>
> [...]
>
> My countrymen, one and all, think calmly and well, upon this whole subject. Nothing valuable can be lost by taking time. ... Intelligence, patriotism, Christianity, and a firm reliance on Him, who has never yet forsaken this favored land, are still competent to adjust, in the best way, all our present difficulty.
>
> In your hands, my dissatisfied fellow countrymen, and not in mine, is the momentous issue of civil war. The government will not assail you. You can have no conflict, without being yourselves the aggressors. You have no oath registered in Heaven to destroy the government, while I shall have the most solemn one to "preserve, protect, and defend" it. (187–88)

The bombardment of Fort Sumter on April 12, 1861 served as the catalyst for the Civil War. It was initiated to preserve the Union. Sandburg delineates how this was the first event of Lincoln's presidency that would test his core beliefs; this was the event that forced Lincoln to act. Beginning in 1861, the dilemma of a divided country would occupy all of Lincoln's time, energy, and thought. It would do the same for the people in this country. This division within the United States would form the principal prism by which Lincoln saw America and the prism by which the people saw themselves. In this regard, *Abraham Lincoln: The*

War Years can be seen as Sandburg's biography of the country—its events, its tragedies, its successes, and its people. Ultimately, it can be seen as a guidebook for Americans living in the twentieth century.

With the careful eye of a journalist, Carl Sandburg begins to describe the unfolding events in America, which led to heightened tension between the North and the South. Sandburg explains how, "After May '61, the U.S. mail service no longer ran into seceded states. In this month too the Confederate Congress authorized those owing debts to the United States to pay the amount of those debts into the Confederate Treasury" (210).

Such details seem to be the strength and the purpose of the biography—re-telling how Lincoln, his colleagues, and his countrymen acted when action had to be taken. It is the people of this country who crowd the book, but so do the many battles, the heightened political tensions, and the personal and collective losses and tragedies. This is what gives Sandburg's second biography of Lincoln its breadth and strength.

With the care of a trained historian, Sandburg covers and catalogs every major detail of the war, including Stephen A. Douglas's post-election support for Lincoln's policy and his support for the anticipated war. Sandburg covers Queen Victoria's May 13, 1861, proclamation of neutrality with regard to the Union and Confederacy. Sandburg also provides details as specific as this: "Out of a total of 1,108 U.S. Army officers, 387 had resigned to go South. These resigned Southerners, 288 of them West Point trained, included promising officers, of actual field and battle service. Among West Pointers in Northern service were 162 born in Slave States" (216). He even reports that Lincoln "queried whether the Southern movement should be called 'secession' or 'rebellion,' saying that the instigators knew the difference" (217).

Throughout the months and years of escalating violence and death, Sandburg traces and details how Lincoln was growing in anxiety but concurrently show-ing a clearer sense of his power and his identity. Sandburg captures this growth incisively when he says, "After nine months as President he was 'I.' Where he had written, 'The executive deems it of importance,' he now wrote, 'I deem it of importance'" (233)

Sandburg also captures the contradictory and complex sentiments of Lincoln's fellow countrymen toward him:

> The organized abolitionists expected little from the President. The execu-tive committee of the American Anti-Slavery Society in its 28th annual report scored Lincoln as "under the delusion that soft words will solve the

nation's sore." They analyzed him: "A sort of bland, respectable middle-
man, between a very modest Right and the most arrogant and exacting
Wrong ... He thinks slavery wrong, but opposes the immediate abolition of
it; believes it ought to be kept out of the Territories, but would admit it to
the Union in new States ... affirms the equality of white men and black in
natural rights but is 'not in favor of negro citizenship'" (233–34).

Sandburg wanted to make clear to readers that Lincoln was gaining a clearer
sense of himself during his years in office, all the while remaining faithful to
the needs of his countrymen. Charting this growth was an essential component
of this biography. Readers would witness this growth and take comfort and
confidence in their own time and in their own country.

But it must be made clear that the bulk of *Abraham Lincoln: The War Years*
is the story of the Civil War, and Civil War historians benefited as much from
the book as did Lincoln historians. Within this discussion, Sandburg presents
Lincoln as a president who followed every minute detail of the war and as a man
whose commitment to the war grew with every passing day. A good example can
be seen in the chapter "Second Bull Run—Antietam—Chaos," when Sandburg
reprints an excerpt from Lincoln's private writings:

I am now stronger with the Army of the Potomac than McClellan. The
supremacy of the civil power has been restored, and the Executive is
again master of the situation. The troops know, that if I made a mistake
in substituting Pope for McClellan, I was capable of rectifying it by again
trusting him. They know, too, that neither Stanton nor I withheld anything
from him at Antietam, and that it was not the administration, but their own
former idol, who surrendered the just results of their terrible sacrifices
and closed the great fight as a drawn battle, when, had he thrown Porter's
corps of fresh men and other available troops upon Lee's army, he would
inevitably have driven it in disorder to the river and captured most of it
before sunset. (265)

Sandburg characterizes Lincoln as a steady and informed commander-in-chief
throughout his years in office. And for Lincoln, nothing came before the war; this
was his absolute focus. The issue of slavery becomes a related factor very soon after
the initiation of the war, but Lincoln's position on slavery, at least as of August 22,
1862, is very clear. In a widely reprinted letter addressed to the country, "probably
reaching nearly all persons in the country who could read" (267), Lincoln wrote:

... I would save the Union. I would save it the shortest way under the Constitution. The sooner the national authority can be restored; the nearer the Union will be "the Union as it was." If there be those who would not save the Union, unless they could at the same time save slavery, I do not agree with them. If there be those would not save the Union unless they could at the same time destroy slavery, I do not agree with them. *My paramount object in this struggle is to save the Union, and is not either to save or to destroy slavery.* If I could save the Union without freeing any slave, I would do it, and if I could save it by freeing some and leaving others alone I would also do that. What I do about slavery, and the colored race, I do because I believe it helps to save the Union; and what I forbear, I forbear because I do not believe it would help to save the Union. (267–68 [italics in original])

Sandburg documents how in the weeks and months that followed the publication of this letter, Lincoln received many letters and visits from prominent African-American and religious leaders, all advocating that Lincoln and Congress take steps to free the slaves. Lincoln changed his mind and his policy. First, he

... signed an act ending Negro slavery in the District of Columbia, the Federal Government to buy the slaves at prices not exceeding $200 each. And, the President wishing it, there was provision for steamship tickets to Liberia or Haiti for any freed slaves who cared to go to those Negro republics. This act of Congress and the President was one of many laws, decisions, new precedents that by percussion and abrasion, by erosion and attrition, were opening gaps in the legal status of slavery, wearing down its props and bulwarks. (270)

With the help of Congress, the Confiscation Act was passed in July of 1862. The law stated that "slaves owned by persons convicted of treason or rebellion should be made free, and furthermore, slaves of rebels who escaped into the Union army lines, or slaves whose masters had run away, or slaves found by the Union Army in places formerly occupied by rebel forces, should all be designated as prisoners of war and set free" (271). Sandburg here presents Lincoln's boldness of character and the boldness of his actions in creating and supporting this policy.

Soon after, Lincoln prepared the Emancipation Proclamation, and with full support of his Cabinet, he justified the act by making the following argument:

... I think the Constitution invests its commander-in-chief with the law of war in time of war. The most that can be said—if so much—is that slaves are property. Is there—has there ever been—any question that by the law of war, property, both of enemies and friends, may be taken when needed? Civilized belligerents do all in their power to help themselves or hurt the enemy, except a few things regarded as barbarous or cruel. (293)

As the war continued into 1863, "the confusion of opinion and action of wartime fell into more regular channels" (318). But the mixed feelings for Lincoln continued to grow, and the war seemed to have no end. The possibility of assassination was a very real threat for Lincoln, and many Americans believed that "the country is marching to its tomb, but the grave-diggers will not confess their crime. … O God! O God! To witness how by the hands of Lincoln-Seward-McClellan, this noblest human structure is crumbled …" (326).

A close reading of Sandburg's biography reveals that Lincoln was always connected with the common people. As a matter of fact, "usually twice a week, on Tuesday evenings at so-called dress receptions and on Saturday evenings at a less formal function, the President met all who came" (335). Having met Lincoln in 1863, Harriet Beecher Stowe wrote the following for her January column of the *Watchman and Reflector* of Boston:

> The world has seen and wondered at the greatest sign and marvel of our day, to-wit, a plain and working man of the people, with no more culture, instruction or education than any such workingman may obtain for himself, called on to conduct the passage of a great people through a crisis involving the destinies of the whole world. ....
>
> Lincoln's strength is of a peculiar kind; it is not aggressive so much as passive, and among passive things it is like the strength not so much of a stone buttress, as of a wire cable. It is strength swaying to every influence, yielding on this side and on that to popular needs, yet tenaciously and inflexibly bound to carry its great end; and probably by no other kind of strength could our national ship have been drawn safely thus far during the tossings and tempests which beset her way. (397)

This characterization of Lincoln embodies Sandburg's presentation of Lincoln as "a plain and working man of the people, with no more culture, instruction or education than any such workingman may obtain for himself, called on to conduct the passage of a great people through a crisis involving the destinies of the whole world. …." If Lincoln could lead a country out of a great crisis, so could men and women survive the difficulties they encountered in Depression America.

But many Americans did not feel this way in the presidential election of 1864, where Lincoln faced George B. McClellan. Sandburg observes that though Lincoln won the electoral vote 212 to 21, "a close study of three states with the largest electoral votes, New York, Pennsylvania and Ohio, showed

Lincoln receiving 930,269 to 843,862 for McClellan, a difference of only 86,407 votes, but giving Lincoln 80 in the Electoral College. Had these three key states by their narrow margin gone for McClellan and been joined by two or three other states, McClellan would have been elected" (503).

In essence, a vote for Lincoln meant a vote for the continuation and support of the Civil War. One month after Lincoln's Second Inaugural Address, and three-and-a-half years after the Civil War began, General Robert E. Lee surrendered his army to Ulysses S Grant on Palm Sunday, April 9, 1865. Over 3,000,000 men in the North and South had seen war service, and 620,000 Americans had died—360,000 from the North, 260,000 from the South (574).

But there was, of course, still tremendous antipathy and opposition to Lincoln in the North as well as the South. One supporter of the Confederate cause was John Wilkes Booth, whose own "Southern heroes almost universally repudiated him as a madman, one who fought foul. And he was that—a lunatic—a diabolically cunning athlete, swordsman, dead shot, horseman, actor. ... His broodings took two directions. He would perform a deed saving the Southern cause while at the same time giving the world a breath-taking dramatic performance" (590–1).

With the death of Lincoln, the nation and the world mourned. In addition, England, France, Germany, Russia, Sweden, Norway, China, and Japan, framed resolutions of condolence, and "to the four corners of the earth began the spread of the Lincoln story and legend" (603). Most of the sermons on April 15, 1865, echoed the sentiments shared by Octavius Brooks Forthingham, pastor of the Third Congregational Unitarian Society in New York:

> The country does not go wild over him; it silently weeps for him; it does not celebrate him as a demigod—it mourns for him as a friend. He let the people work through him; and in his own esteem held a high place enough when he acted as an organ and an instrument. Such humility almost passes understanding—it runs into self-forgetfulness; it borders even on saintliness. He hoped little, expected nothing. A man of low temperament and sad nature, he worked and waited, waited and worked, bearing all things, enduring all things, but neither believing all things nor all things happening; bearing and enduring oh how much! even from his friends. What a history was written on that careworn and furrowed face—of suffering accepted, sorrow entertained, emotions buried, and duty done! (599–600)

This is the characterization that Sandburg wanted to capture in his biography, one of a man who "let the people work through him; and in his own esteem held a high place enough when he acted as an organ and an instrument."

In thousands of commentaries, Lincoln incarnated two ideals—"Emancipation and Union" (604). Sandburg adds that "Out of the smoke and stench, out of the music and violet dreams of war, Lincoln stood perhaps taller than any other of the many great heroes. This was in the mind of many. None threw a longer shadow than he. And to him the great hero was 'the People.' He could not say too often that he was merely their instrument" (605).

Sandburg concludes the biography by re-tracing the 1,700-mile route of the Lincoln funeral train back to Lincoln's hometown, Springfield, Illinois. In all, tens of thousands of Americans were on hand to see the funeral train as it took Lincoln back home. He was buried on May 4, 1865, at Oak Ridge Cemetery. Sandburg concludes the biography poetically:

> And the night came with great quiet.
> And there was rest.
> The prairie years, the war years, were over. (611)

Carl Sandburg's *Abraham Lincoln: The Prairie Years* and *Abraham Lincoln: The War Years* celebrated the theme of "the People," and it gave Sandburg the freedom to take history and transform it into a new type of imaginative fiction. With the Lincoln books, Sandburg perfected his deep immersion into American culture, American folklore and myth, American history, and into the spirit of American people. This journey into the country's past, present, and future produced a related body of works, which help to form the magnum opus of Carl Sandburg's America. (Between the period of the publication of these two books, Sandburg also published two very powerful and related works of poetry, *Good Morning, America* [1928] and *The People, Yes* [1936]. Sandburg also used the model of historical fiction for his only and very ambitious novel, *Remembrance Rock*, published in 1948.)

It is also important to note that Abraham Lincoln remained a perpetual subject of interest for Sandburg, and for decades after the publication of the two biographies Americans connected Carl Sandburg's name with Lincoln's. Often, Sandburg's university circuit readings and television and radio performances included prose, poetic, or musical tributes to Lincoln. Additionally, "he had made a startling discovery about the relatively new medium of television in 1954 when he had been paid five thousand dollars to read his *Lincoln Preface* on Lincoln's birthday" (Sandburg, *The Prairie Years and The War Years* 638). From that point on, Sandburg often used his television performances to tell his story of Lincoln. In essence, Carl Sandburg became Lincoln's "most visible ambassador in the twentieth century" (Niven 680), and America knew that his name was deeply entwined with Lincoln's. As one of the relatively few private citizens to ever address Congress, Sandburg was asked to read some words about Lincoln to a Joint Session in 1959.

The figure of Abraham Lincoln united Sandburg to "the People"; every book published after 1926 can be seen as an additional statement about their place, their significance, and their purpose in American life. Sandburg hoped that Lincoln would serve as the archetypal man to every American living in the twentieth century, providing the blueprint of morality and behavior to instruct them on how to resolve the new problems facing mankind.

Finally, the two Lincoln biographies should be seen as the cornerstone for Sandburg's project of nation-building. Sandburg stresses Lincoln's belief in the basic rights of man, and characterizes him as the archetypal common man. The biographies also provide a different experience of history, and offer twentieth-century readers an optimistic view of the future; in them Lincoln becomes the representative figure of an entire nation. There is little doubt that Sandburg gave the sixteenth president new life and made him meaningful and relevant in the twentieth century.

Since the publication of Sandburg's two separate biographies of Lincoln, scores of scholarly books focusing Lincoln's morality and spirituality have appeared. One of the best is Stewart Winger's *Lincoln, Religion, and Romantic Cultural Politics* (2003) which explains how William E. Barton's *The Soul of Abraham Lincoln* (1920) created "a tradition of religious biography" (Winger 6). This, in turn, led to a significant number of books that exclusively focused on Lincoln's interior and religious life.

Published in 2002 by the University Press of Mississippi, James Tackach *Lincoln's Moral Vision: The Second Inaugural Address* (2002) argues that

> the 701-word Second Inaugural, delivered sixteen months after Lincoln's remarks at Gettysburg and only forty-two days before his death, is, in many ways, the more revealing [speech], if not the more stylistically pleasing, speech—more revealing because the later speech discloses Lincoln's thinking, at the end of his life, on key issues with which he had grappled throughout his long political career: slavery and race, the meaning of nationhood, the purpose of government, the role of God in the universe. (xiv)

Tackach's very careful and insightful study helps readers gain insight into the same Lincoln that Sandburg aimed to present in his biography. Tackach goes on to explain how

> The Lincoln presented in this study is a mere mortal, shaped by the attitudes of his time and place, who lived what Plato's Socrates would have called the examined life and who, in doing so, grappled in a moving way with the key issues of his countrymen and countrywomen in some of the most poignant prose delivered by an American president. The Lincoln of this study is a complex man with a remarkable mind who defies the easy categorization attempted by some who have written about Lincoln. (xiv–xv)

Tackach's book clarifies and confirms what Nicolay and Hay articulated in their own Lincoln biography of 1890:

> In the four years since he had assumed the presidency, Lincoln had greatly broadened his war aims. No longer were victory and political reunifications his only objectives. He now set his sights on the greater task of the moral reconstruction of the nation. (Adler 555)

Currently, over 40,000 books on Abraham Lincoln have been published, and there are many more to come. Sandburg's Lincoln is likely to keep its unique place among them.

Chapter 9

Transcontinental Poet: Carl Sandburg Celebrates the Common Man and America's Story

I don't want writers, I want fighters.

—Henry Justin Smith, Editor of the [Chicago]
Daily News and Sandburg's hero (qtd. in Mitgang 127)

The trouble is that writers are too damned literary—too damned literary. There has grown up—Swinburne I think an apostle of it—the doctrine (you have heard of it? it is dinned everywhere), art for art's sake: think of it—art for art's sake. Let a man really accept that—let that really be his ruling—and he is lost ...

Instead of regarding literature as only a weapon, an instrument, in the service of something larger than itself, it looks upon itself as an end—as a fact to be finally worshipped, adored. To me that's all a horrible blasphemy—a bad smelling apostasy.

—a remark of Walt Whitman to Horace Traubel,
his friend and secretary, reported in
The Seven Arts in 1917 (qtd. in Aaron 7)

B eginning with the Abraham Lincoln biography of 1926, Carl Sandburg endeavored to transform America into a place of promise and hope, and with absolute resoluteness, in all of his literary works published thereafter, he begins to build on the theme of "the People." In many ways, Sandburg's vision of America incarnates Lincoln's vision—one deeply imbued with ideals of national unity and patriotism, as well as a sincere and committed concern for the disenfranchised. Sandburg's post-1920 works become much more exciting when they are culturally contextualized because he was one of few "serious" writers celebrating this country and its common people. There were no vicious attacks on small town life; with the exception of *The People, Yes,* his poetry and prose did not articulate themes of cultural fracture; and his intended audience always remained, not the philosophical elite, but the common man. There is also little doubt that with the publication of his first Lincoln biography, Sandburg developed a firmer grasp of what he wanted his poetry and prose to achieve. The letter he wrote to Romain Rolland in October of 1919 articulates his sense of purpose:

> I wonder if I make myself clear in venturing to suggest that I am for reason and satire, religion and propaganda, violence and assassination, or force and syndicalism, any of them, in the extent and degree to which it will serve a purpose of the people at a given time toward the establishment eventually of the control of the means of life by the people. (qtd. in Mitgang 172)

Not surprisingly, this directly echoes Bill Haywood's 1912 message insisting that "… no socialist can be a law-abiding citizen" (Aron 13). And it also directly echoes Sandburg's 1918 article published in the *International Socialist Review* titled "Haywood of the I.W.W." In the article, Sandburg deifies Haywood and compares him to John Brown:

> So Big Bill Haywood, nearly sixty years later, appears in history, another man dominated by a dream. Haywood has a vision of industrial democracy established, a hope of security and justice for all the workers of the world, the shackles of capitalist wage slavery struck off. How is this vision to be attained? Thru [sic] a world wide general strike of the working class, thru mass action of the working people of the world, without violence necessarily, without death penalties, revenges and punitive indemnities. Merely thru a folding of arms, a refusal to make or transport the goods of the world, till the autocracies yielded to a newer order. (*Modern American Poetry*, par. 4)

But Sandburg knew that social change and "industrial democracy" would not come "thru [sic] a [mere] folding of arms." As a writer, he had work to do.

As noted earlier, a close examination of Sandburg's post-1922 period reveals him ambitiously and actively participating in multiple genres, including song, children's story, poem, novel, and biography. The thread that connects all of these publications, though, reveals a tenacious preoccupation with the theme of "the People"—and all of Sandburg's works can be seen as his way of taking "direct action."

Not surprisingly, "the People" in America overwhelmingly responded to Sandburg and his message. Beginning with the publication of *Rootabaga Stories* in 1922, as mentioned in chapter two, Sandburg enjoyed what would become a very long career of astonishingly significant book sales, concurrently giving hundreds of radio and television appearances and delivering scores of public readings. With his message of hope and optimism and his sincere and committed faith in "the People," Carl Sandburg would become one of the most successful and celebrated writers of his time.

Carl Sandburg's study of Lincoln gave him the freedom to take history and transform it, and it also reflected his deep, life-long immersion in American culture, folklore and myth, and national history. This journey into the country's past and his participation in the present allowed him to speculate about the future. This journey ultimately produced a related body of poetry and prose works that help to form the magnum opus of Carl Sandburg's America—his greatest achievement, and, I would argue, one of the most unfairly neglected achievements of the twentieth century.

This chapter will explore the varied ways Carl Sandburg presents and celebrates the theme of "the People" in his post-Lincoln works, an issue in Sandburg scholarship that has not been sufficiently appreciated or assessed. A careful study of this period of Sandburg's output will also reveal a varied literary richness that has long been overlooked by scholars of American literature. Finally, a close study of this period will reveal a complex and evolving political ideology at the center of specific works, which include *The American Songbag* (1927), *Good Morning, America* (1928), *The People, Yes* (1936), and *Remembrance Rock* (1948). Aside from *Abraham Lincoln: The War Years* (1939), these four publications constitute the major works Sandburg published after 1922.

Central to this discussion is an idea offered in Heinrich Straumann's *American Literature in the Twentieth Century*. In the chapter titled "The Fate of Man," Straumann explains how

A considerable part of modern American literature arises from the fundamental question "What is Man?" If this question is put into a pragmatic or deterministic point of view it inevitably changes into the one "How does Man behave within the given surroundings?" ... a great number of very prominent American writers obviously take a point of view that is neither pragmatic nor determinist but which appears to be connected with other elements of human thought. Some of them are plainly interested in Man's destiny in the infinite, and if they are philosophers, their concern is often with those values that philosophical idealism or Christian tradition have accepted as a basis for the understanding of Man's position in the universe. Thinkers like Josiah Royce, Paul Elmer More, Reinhold

Neibuhr, Paul Tillich, a poet like T. S. Eliot, and a dramatist and novelist like Thornton Wilder, would have to be mentioned here. Another group such as Sherwood Anderson, William Faulkner, and others tries to approach the mystery of Man by probing as deeply as possible into all the hidden recesses of his soul. And a third group appears to be trying to bridge the gulf between the conception of a hard reality and a vision of the meaning of life and death, as well as to search for new values. This is the field of writers such as Hemingway, Thomas Wolfe, Steinbeck, Robert Penn Warren, and a number of others. (71)

Beginning in 1926—with the publication of the Lincoln biography—Sandburg's works set out on this very complex and ambitious quest of discovering and articulating "the fate of man." Like Hemingway, Wolfe, Steinbeck, and Robert Penn Warren, Sandburg belongs to this third group, aiming "to bridge the gulf between the conception of a hard reality and a vision of the meaning of life and death, as well as to search for new values." And for Sandburg, the theme of "the People" would serve as the central way to unpack and understand "the fate of man" he saw.

Beginning with *Abraham Lincoln: The Prairie Years*, Sandburg's writing offers synthesis and resolution. Sandburg's intended audience always remains "the People" of this country, and he looks to great figures in American history (Lincoln) and to the most significant historical events to shed light on his view concerning "the fate of man." For Sandburg, "the fate of man" hinges on "the People" recognizing and understanding the sustained achievements of their role as the cornerstone buttressing the economy and the healthy growth of this country. But the concept of "the fate of man" equally hinges on the privileged socioeconomic group in this country, also recognizing that "the People" should be accurately recognized as the foundation of the American economy and valued for their day-to-day contributions.

Not unlike the New Humanism of Paul Elmer More in the 1920s, which "stressed the importance of personal integrity and personality as the essential components of a society which itself is more important than the sum total of individuals" (Straumann 73), Sandburg's Lincoln biography serves as the quintessential work embodying this very idea. For Sandburg, collective society was indeed "more important than the sum total of individuals." *The American Songbag* (1927), *Good Morning, America* (1928), *The People, Yes* (1936), and *Remembrance Rock* (1948) illustrate this point. With the exception of *Remembrance Rock* and the Lincoln biographies, there are no main characters in Sandburg's works except for "the People."

In addition, Sandburg's post-1920 works offer a "new way of formulating old problems and of establishing a link between metaphysical questions and personal experience" (78). In essence, as a Socialist turned pragmatist, Sandburg was attempting to reconcile and resolve the cultural fracture he was witnessing in the 1920s and the economic fracture of the 1930s.

Essential to this discussion is an awareness of the radical political literary climate out of which Sandburg was emerging. The "Preface" of Daniel Aaron's touchstone *Writers on the Left: Episodes in American Literary Communism* (1961) makes the central point that

> A very small fraction of the Left Wing Writers were once members of the Communist Party. A considerably larger number might better be designated "fellow travelers." I apply this slippery and inexact phrase to those who were in the "movement," who sympathized with the objectives of the party, wrote for the party press, or knowingly affiliated with associations sponsored by the party. Without including the fellow travelers or liberals or nonparty radicals, the story of literary communism would be very thin indeed, for the Communist Party had far less influence on writers than the idea of Communism or the image of Soviet Russia. (ix)

Aaron goes on to discuss the "four radicals" of the movement—Max Eastman, Floyd Dell, John Reed, and Randolph Bourne (individuals Sandburg knew well)—and argues that these men, and a handful of literary figures, were "more deeply moved by a social vision, and became committed to revolution" (Aaron 12). Aaron also makes the incisive point that

> Among the contending radical philosophies, anarchism and syndicalism appealed more to young artist-rebels than the more staid versions of socialism, and the activists in the revolutionary movement—Gene Debs, Big Bill Haywood, Emma Goldman, Mother Jones, for example, seemed closer to the spirit of the artist's rebellion than the white-collar bread-and-butter theorists. Middle-class socialism of the Ruskinian sort or the bureaucratic practical business-socialism of Victor Berger and Morris Hillquit were tame compared to flamboyant programs of direct action and dynamite or proclamations announcing the supremacy of the individual and voluntary co-operation. (Aaron 13)

Daniel Aaron also makes the claim that "Socialist art had to forge its own tools to express its own culture" (Aaron 15). To understand this point, it is important to examine Max Eastman's *Venture*, a novel that takes Big Bill Haywood as its protagonist. In the novel, Haywood carefully explains why there is no proletarian art for the Pittsburgh steelworker and articulates and adumbrates on what workers' art will be like:

> "Not only is art impossible to such a man," he said, "but life is impossible. He does not live. He just works. He does the work that enables you to live. He does the work that enables you to enjoy art, and to make it, and to have a nice meeting like this and talk it over."
>
> Bill used "nice" without irony; he meant it.
>
> "The only problem, then, about proletarian art," he continued, "is how to make it possible, how to make life possible to the proletariat. In solving that problem we should be glad of your understanding, but we don't ask your help. We are going to solve it at your expense. Since you have got life, and we have got nothing but work, we are going to take our share of life away from you, and put you to work."
>
> "I suppose you will want to know what my ideal of proletarian art is," he continued, "what I think it will be like, when a revolution brings it into existence. I think it will be very much kindlier than your art. There will be a social spirit in it. Not so much boasting about personality. Artists won't be so egotistical. The highest ideal of an artist will be to write a song which the workers will sing, to compose a drama which the great throngs of workers can perform out of doors. When we stop fighting each other—for wages of existence on one side, and for unnecessary luxury on the other—then perhaps we shall all become human beings and surprise ourselves with the beautiful things we do and make on the earth." (qtd. in Aaron 16)

Sandburg was quite familiar with the theories of the Socialist Party of America (after all, he had been a card-carrying member of the Party since 1908). He also knew the works of Henry James and John Dewey, but his personal relationships with Big Bill Haywood and Eugene V. Debs possibly had a more powerful impact on his writing.

After 1922, with renewed and absolute commitment, Sandburg began creating an American brand of proletarian art. He would try "to make it [art] possible, and make life possible for the proletariat" (Aaron 16). Beginning with *Rootabaga Stories*, everything Sandburg published was not only, as Big Bill Haywood had said, "kindlier," but it had "a social spirit in it." And this was only too natural for Sandburg, who had for years, even into the early and mid-1920s, written for Socialist publications, including *The Masses*—"that spectacular organ of socialism, anarchism, paganism, and rebellion" (Aaron 18).

Chapter 10

Teaching America Its Songs: The American Songbag

O ne overarching and consistent thread that appears in Sandburg's post-1922 publications is his interest in folklore and myth, which is manifested throughout his volumes of poetry and prose, most conspicuously perhaps in *The American Songbag* (1927)—Sandburg's collection celebrating popular song. Sandburg wanted to make life more meaningful for the proletariat, and what better way than to document its songs? In one sense, *The American Songbag* was to preserve the art of common people—the "masses" of the Socialists.

In the *Columbia Literary History of the United States* (1988), Cary Nelson maintains that among the "poetries" in need of critical appraisal are Black poetry, poetry by women, the poetry of popular song, and the poetry of mass social movements. Since 1988, when Nelson made his appeal, significant strides have been made in the recovery of Black poetry and poetry by women. Currently, interest in both of these poetries is very strong, as evidenced in what now seems to be the permanent presence of many Black and women poets in college-level literature anthologies, as well as in the proliferation of books that focus on the literatures previously marginalized.

But the poetry of popular song and the poetry of mass social movements, both of which are central to the literary history of America (and to Sandburg's literary project), deserve equal attention. They deserve to be understood because they played a powerful and central role in the changing lives of average working Americans. We must remember that the period from 1890 to 1920 witnessed a rapidly changing way of life—from rural to urban—as well as the exponential growth of capitalism. This period also saw a widening chasm between the rich and the poor, which led to bitter conflict between labor and capital. In his book *We Shall Be All: A History of the Industrial Workers of the World* (1969), Melvyn Dubofsky describes the period from 1890 to 1920 as the "era of populism, progressivism, and the rise of American Socialism: The Age of Reform" (Dubofsky

6). For the first time in history, America saw what Morris Hillquit describes as "the development of fixed and permanent economic classes" (Hillquit 20). For the poets of popular song and mass social movements, as well as for many other politically-conscious writers, chiefly Carl Sandburg, these themes and subjects became and remained a central focus of their works.

Cary Nelson points to Joe Hill's *Little Red Song Book* (1909), published by the Industrial Workers of the World (IWW), as a groundbreaking work of both popular song and social protest. The leadership of the IWW believed that "abstract doctrine meant nothing to the disinherited; specific grievances meant everything!" (Dubofsky 90). In addition, the IWW believed in confronting concrete problems caused by industrial life. Like Bill Haywood, who divided "all the world into three parts: the capitalists, who are the employing class that makes money out of money; the skilled laborers; and the masses" (Dubofsky 87). Sandburg's poetry and prose consistently make significant reference to this same socioeconomic division in American society.

When Sandburg elected to begin his work on *The American Songbag* in the early 1920s, he was building on a literary tradition that was associated with social protest. At this point in his career, he understood himself as a committed political writer and was developing a reputation as a cultural patriot. Unlike Sigmund Spaeth's *Read 'Em and Weep* (1927), a very popular songbook of the 1920s and 1930s that collected sentimental songs about home and family, and songs that taught a moral and promoted proper values of patriotism, industry, cleanliness, and reverence for God, Sandburg's book—much like the *Little Red Songbook*—collected the songs of "Sailors, Negroes, Hoboes, Prisoners, Workers, the romantic heroes of the American Left" (xi). Sandburg's book featured a group of Americans not mentioned in Spaeth's book, and Sandburg "labored mightily to bring folk art to the masses and save them from commercial exploiters who would sell them the confections of Tin Pan Alley" (*American Songbag* ix). This was Sandburg's first effort to bring art to the masses, to celebrate the music of "the People" in this country. This would be a tradition-shattering text because, in essence, Sandburg's book of songs was seen by many as a subversive effort to further romanticize the life of the common man.

In a letter dated January 26, 1921, to Isadora Bennett Reed, a former colleague of Sandburg's on the (Chicago) *Daily News*, who lived in Columbia, South Carolina, and began to send him plantation songs, Sandburg articulated much of the purpose of his songbook:

> Thank you many ways for those songs. You know how to put 'em down. This whole thing is only in its beginnings, America knowing its songs ... It's been amazing to me to see how audiences rise to 'em; how the lowbrows just naturally like Frankie an' Albert while the highbrows, with the explanation that the murder and adultery is less in percentage than in the average grand opera, and it is the equivalent for America of the famous gutter songs of Paris—they get it.
>
> Understand, a new song learnt is worth more to me than any Jap print or rare painting. I can take it into a railroad train or a jail or anywhere. (qtd. in Mitgang 196–97)

This line directly echoes Big Bill Haywood's discussion of proletarian art in Max Eastman's *Venture:* "The highest ideal of the artist will be to write a song which the workers will sing, to compose a drama which great throngs of workers can perform out of doors" (qtd. in Aaron 16).

If the purpose of *Abraham Lincoln: The Prairie Years* was to acquaint Americans with its nation's past and with one of the greatest figures that ever walked the earth, the goal of this new work was to allow "America to know its songs," the songs "the People" sang.

In a letter to Vachel Lindsay dated April 6, 1927, Sandburg acknowledges how his songbook is a compilation of America and its people:

> Just now I am trying to finish up "The American Songbag." It has mounted beyond all first plans for it. It is not so much my book as that of a thousand other people who have made its 260 colonial, pioneer, railroad, work-gang, hobo, Irish, Negro, Mexican gutter, Gossamer songs, chants and ditties ... (qtd. in Mitgang 246–47)

And in letters to H. L. Mencken and Helen Keller, Sandburg explains how the production of *The American Songbag* "would be a thankless job and my gratification about the book is merely as that of a patriot who has seen duty and done it" (qtd. in Mitgang 257). He also describes the work as "panoramic, tumultuous, transcontinental" (qtd. in Mitgang 270).

Garrison Keillor observes that the work was compiled by Sandburg and "his friends from coast to coast and from the Gulf to Canada" (*American Songbag* vii). The book contains singable words and music—complete harmonizations or piano accompaniments to 290 songs. Sandburg subdivided the book into chapters with titles like "Mexican Border Songs," "Minstrel Songs," "Bandit Biographies," "Tarnished Love Tales," "Pioneer Memories," and "Darn Fool Ditties." In an incisive description of the 1927 publication, Sandburg wrote:

> The song history of America ... will accomplish two things. It will give the
> feel and atmosphere, the layout, the lingo, of regions, of breeds of men,
> of customs and slogans, in a manner and air not given in regular history,
> to be read and not sung. And besides such a history would require that the
> student sing his way through most of the chapters. (vii)

In essence, the *American Songbag* is the history of America as told in song. In the December 1927 issue of the *Nation*, Mark Van Doren, a consistent advocate of Sandburg's works, pointed out a connection between Sandburg's songbook and his biography of Lincoln. He explained how "Sandburg's Lincoln biography and this collection have a common origin in his feeling that contemporary American poetry, perhaps including his own, was not getting at the heart of the people. This collection is a contribution to American history in an entirely serious sense" (qtd. in Salwak 29). Again, as Daniel Aaron mentions in *Writers on the Left*, "Socialist art had to forge its own tools to express its own culture." Sandburg knew that the conventions governing different genres had to be broken because "the People" in this country had a right to art that was accessible. But Sandburg knew that he was taking a chance with his brand of "Socialist art."

Conard Aiken—a harsh critic of Sandburg during most of his career—described the songbook as "a book about the America Sandburg loves. But these folk songs are at the lowest level, reflecting spiritual poverty in their crudeness" (qtd. in Salwak 30). In many ways, this is true. Sandburg did concern himself with capturing the songs of the lower classes—the working men and women of this country—"the People." These were songs never collected before; for decades, these songs had been a part of an oral tradition, and Sandburg, seeing himself as a cultural spokesman for the lower classes, took it upon himself to leave a permanent record of them. He also saw this work as an opportunity to celebrate and, more importantly, (re)introduce this world of song to all America. Sandburg became a kind of folk minstrel who not only collected but "performed them [the songs of the people] to such an extent that more and more Negro songs and songs of laborers and convicts, plains and mountains were brought to the attention of music publishers and radio and television media" (Callahan, *Carl Sandburg* 105). And for the next thirty years, in the thousands of live performances Sandburg gave across the country, he performed these songs.

If we closely examine Sandburg's *The American Songbag*, several striking characteristics stand out. First, the work "marshals the genius of thousands of original singing Americans" (*American Songbag* xii), and it is enhanced by meticulous annotations and prefatory notes indicating where the songs originated and how they changed through the years. For example, in the section titled "Hobo Songs," Sandburg includes the song "Hallelujah, I'm a Bum." In his prefatory note, he says:

> This old song heard at the water tanks of railroads in Kansas in 1897 and from harvest hands who worked in the wheat fields of Pawnee County, was picked up later by the I.W.W.'s, who made verses of their own from it, and gave it wide fame. The migratory workers are familiar with the Salvation Army missions, and have adopted the Army custom of occasionally abandoning all polite formalities and striking deep into the common things and ways for their music and words. A "handout" is food handed out from a back door as distinguished from "a sit down" which means an entrance into a house and a chair at a table. (*American Songbag* 184)

Sandburg himself said in his Introduction to the book:

> A wide human procession marches through these pages. The rich and the poor; robbers, murderers, hangmen; fathers and wild boys; mothers with soft words for their babies; workmen on railroads, steamboats, ships; wanderers and lovers of homes, tell what life has done to them. Love and hate in many patterns and designs, heart cries of high and low pitch, are in these verses and tunes ... With more people than ever taking to folk songs, some believe these songs have a relation to faith in the people, that there is involved an instinct or feeling related to the importance of songs arising out of the people. (qtd in Callahan, *Carl Sandburg* 106–07)

Sandburg's book would serve as a powerful articulation that helped to further the program of the writers who saw themselves as writing on the Left.

The first section of *The American Songbag*, titled "Dramas and Portraits," includes the "Boll Weevil Song." This song—known well to farmers and ranchers in Texas—captures the "billion dollar devastations of this little eater of cotton crops [that] are of America's traditions of tragedy" (8). A few pages later appears a song titled "John Henry," a song about a man in a southern work-camp gang who lives a simple life and is equally committed to his work as well as to the many women in his life:

1 John Henry tol' his cap'n
Dat a man wuz a natural man,
An' befo' he'd let dat steam drill run him down,
He'd fall dead wid a hammer in his han'
He'd fall dead wid a hammer in his han'

2 Cap'n he sez to John Henry:
"Gonna bring me a steam drill 'round;
Take that steel drill out on the job,
Gonna whop that steel on down
Gonna whop that steel on down."

3 John Henry sez to his cap'n:
"Send me a twele-poun' hammer aroun',
A twelve-poun' hammer wid a fo'-foot handle,
An' I beat yo' steam drill down
An' I beat yo' steam drill down." (25–6)

As the song continues, John Henry dies, and readers eventually meet his infant son and the several women with whom he maintained relationships. Each of these women comments on her love for John Henry, but the last woman to speak explains how she "got that dress" and "dose shoes so fine." She relates how she "got dat dress" from "a railroad man" and "dose shoes so fine" from "a driver in a mine" (25). All of the characters in Sandburg's songs are very real people, with very real lives. And many of them, as is the case with John Henry, saw themselves reacting against the industrial technology of the time and preferred to be "natural" men.

Sandburg's book is valuable for other reasons. His decision to include a section titled "Revolutionary Love Tales or Colonial and Revolutionary Antiques" show his interest in songs that belong to a genre that was largely forgotten at the time, and Sandburg captures the words and melodies of these songs. In the introductory note to the section titled "The Lincolns and the Hankses," Sandburg relates how "A famous oblong song book of the pioneer days in the Middle West was 'The Missouri Harmony,' published in 1808 by Morgan and Sanxay of Cincinnati. Young Abraham Lincoln and his sweetheart, Ann Rutledge, sang from this book in the Rutledge tavern in New Salem, according to old settlers there" (152). The chapter is devoted to songs that Abraham Lincoln would have heard during his lifetime and also includes two "campaign ditties of 1860" which "have the brag and extravaganza of electioneering," (167) titled "Lincoln and Liberty" and "Old Abe Lincoln Came Out of the Wilderness."

There are also many songs in *The American Songbag* which focus on marginalized social misfits and outcasts, including "Cocaine Lil," whose life was spent, and ended, using cocaine. Other songs, like "Seven Long Years in State Prison" and "Been in the Pen So Long," tell the stories of criminals, one of which has spent "Seven long years in prison,/For knocking a man down the alley and taking his gold watch and chain" (218). Sections titled "Hobo Songs," "The

Big Brutal City," "Railroad and Work Gangs," and "Bandit Biographies" are included. The book concludes with a section titled "Road To Heaven." These songs include "Jesus, Won't You Come B'm-By?," which is one of the "longest lasting creations of the Negro of slave days" (469). Also included is "God's Goin' to Set This World on Fire"—a Negro spiritual IWW members "often made jail walls ring with" (478). Most of the songs in this section, though, can be classified as "Negro Spirituals."

North Callahan points out (in 1987) that "the recent revival of folk music among young people in the United States and elsewhere was spurred by Carl Sandburg more than is generally realized" (Callahan, *Carl Sandburg* 105), and Bing Crosby echoed this sentiment in "a handwritten foreword to the 1950 edition [of *The American Songbag*]." He wrote, "American music lovers owe Carl Sandburg a great debt for the ceaseless research which has rediscovered so much authentic American music for their enjoyment" (qtd. in Callahan, *Carl Sandburg* 107). From 1927 into the late 1940s, the songs in *The American Songbag* were brought to life in Carl Sandburg's performances. Sandburg's poetry and prose readings were often interspersed with songs from the collection. William Allen White once described a Sandburg performance thus:

> The Carl Sandburg entertainment is more than a lecture. It is a concert, a grand opera, philosophic pabulum and dramatic entertainment all in one. I have never enjoyed an evening's entertainment more. I can recommend it to the highbrow or the lowbrow, if any, without stint, let or hindrance. (qtd. in Callahan, *Carl Sandburg* 107)

Chapter 11

Sandburg Celebrates America in His Later Poetry—
Good Morning, America

Working eighteen-hour days, traveling across the country giving hundreds of performances, and running himself physically and mentally ragged, in October of 1928, just a few months after the publication of his songbook, fifty-year-old Carl Sandburg published one of his most critically acclaimed books of poetry—*Good Morning, America.*

Reverberating with the spirit of *Abraham Lincoln: The Prairie Years* and *The American Songbag,* Sandburg's volume of poetry, once again, takes a panoramic and sweeping view of America, its places, and its people. The theme of the book—which loosely threads it together—appears in section nineteen of the opening title poem when Sandburg is addressing a personified version of America:

> You have kissed good-by to one century, one little priceless album.
> You will yet kiss good-by to ten, twenty centuries. Ah! You shall have such albums!
> Your mothers, America, have labored and carried harvests of generations—
> Across the spillways come further harvests, new tumultuous populations,
> Young strangers, crying, "We are here! We belong! look at us!"
> Good morning, America! (*Complete Poems* 335)

The entire volume is a study of this country's past, present, future, but it equally concerns itself with the country's folklore and its everyday working people. In section six of the title poem, Sandburg recounts "the figures of heroes set up as memorials, testimonies of fact" (323)—including statues dispersed across the country—statues of Leif Ericson, Columbus, George Washington, Andrew Jackson, Ulysses S Grant, Robert E. Lee, and Abraham Lincoln. About Lincoln, though, he explains how, unlike the others, his "memory is kept in a living, arterial highway moving across state/lines from coast to coast to the murmur, Be good to each other, sisters; don't fight brothers" (323).

Section nine begins with a description of the industrial revolution in this country, and goes on to describe how "the talk runs" and how "the latest/songs go from Broadway west across the country—the latest/movies go from Hollywood east across the country" (327). Section eleven catalogs "the proverbs of the people." Seen in its totality, this untitled twenty-page poem, containing twenty-one interconnected divisions, frames the theme of the entire work—America and its people.

A group titled "Corn Belt" includes poems like "She Opens the Barn Door Every Morning," describing a farm woman who uneventfully milks the cows every morning. "Field People" offers a view of a landscape where people spend their days working, only to disappear forever:

> How the field people go away.
> The corn row people, the toadflux, mushroom,
> Thistlebloom people,
> How they rise, sing songs they learn, and then go away,
> Leaving in the air no last will and testament at all,
> Leaving no last whisper at all on how this sister,
> That brother, this friend, such and such a sweetheart
> Is remembered with a gold leaf, a cup rainbow home,
> A cricket's hut for counting its summer heartbeats,
> A caught shimmer of one haunted moonray to be passed on—
> The running southwest wind knows them all.
> (*Complete Poems* 345–46)

Just like the songs that appear in page after page of *The American Songbag*, every poem in *Good Morning, America* can be seen as a work of proletarian art. As Bill Haywood said in Max Eastman's *Venture*, "There will be a social spirit in it [the new workers' art]" (Aaron 16).

Indeed, several radical poems also appear to support Sandburg's committed goal of "Revolution." "Again?" indicts "Old Man Woolworth" and his dream to build "the biggest building in the world," and Sandburg also makes it clear that the cost of the building was funded by

> ... women buying mousetraps,
> Wire cloth dishrags, ten-cent sheet music,
> They paid for it; the electric tower
> Might yell an electric sign to the inbound
> Ocean liners, "Look what the washerwomen
> Of America can do with their nickels," or
> "See what a nickel and a dime can do" ... (368)

In this poem, Sandburg is reminding readers that the power ultimately lies in the hands of "the People." They are the ones who allow the American economy to continue moving forward, and their labor and their consumerism allow the wealthiest people in society to live lives of splendor and extravagance.

Another poem that functions as a piece of scathing social criticism is titled "Landscape":

> On a mountain-side the real estate agents
> Put up signs marking the city lots to be sold there.
> A man whose father and mother were Irish
> Ran a goat farm half-way down the mountain;
> He drove a covered wagon years ago,
> Understood how to handle a rifle,
> Shot grouse, buffalo, Indians, in a single year,
> And now was raising goats around a shanty.
> Down at the foot of the mountain
> Two Japanese families had flower farms.
> A man and woman were in rows of sweet peas
> Picking the pink and white flowers
> To put in baskets and take to the Los Angeles market.
> They were clean as what they handled
> There in the morning sun, the big people and baby-faces.
> Across the road high on another mountain
> Stood a house saying, "I am it," a commanding house.
> There was the home of a motion picture director
> Famous for lavish doll house interiors,
> Clothes ransacked from the latest designs for women
> In the combats of "male against female."
> The mountain, the scenery, the layout of the landscape,
> And the peace of the morning sun as it happened,
> The miles of houses pocketed in the valley beyond—
> It was all worth looking at, worth wondering about,
> How long it might last, how young it might be.
> [Hollywood 1923] (*Complete Poems* 420–21 [brackets in original])

This poem captures the economic shift that was taking place in America. Land that used to belong to a "man whose father and mother were Irish" is still able to furnish an independent living, and the "Two Japanese families" also use the land to make their living. Sandburg juxtaposes this agrarianism with the "motion picture director"—who never has, and never will, use the land to make a living. For Sandburg, "the mountain, the scenery, the layout of the landscape … was all worth looking at, worth wondering about." He concludes the poem in such a way that prompts readers to reflect on the radical economic changes and the shift in land ownership that has taken place over a generation. Additionally, readers are asked to ponder "how long it might last." Sandburg, thus, has readers consider these important questions: "Is this the direction America is headed? Is this a sign of things to come?"

All of the poems in *Good Morning, America* are simple and straightforward. They focus on the commonplace. Poems like "Webs" allow readers to think about the issue of determinism versus fate. Sandburg writes:

> Every man spins a web of light circles
> And hangs this web in the sky
> Or finds it hanging, already hung for him,
> Written as a path for him to travel.
> The white spiders know how this geography goes.
> Their feet tell them when to spin,
> How to weave in a criss-cross
> Among elms and maples, among radishes and button weeds,
> Among cellar timbers and old shanty doors.
> Not only the white spiders, also the yellow and the blue,
> Also the black and purple spiders
> Listen when their feet tell them to spin one.
> And while every spider spins a web of light circles
> Or finds one already hung for him,
> So does every man born under the sky. (*Complete Poems* 426)

Here, Sandburg takes a philosophical idea and frames it in everyday terms. This kind of poem, representative of a significant majority of poems in the volume, encourages the everyday working man who reads it to think about complex philosophical ideas. In essence, Sandburg is working with a provocative contemporary idea intellectuals were wrestling with at the time, and he reduces that idea to its very core by using an example from the natural world. The purpose of this transformation is to bring the idea closer to "the People." Ultimately, Sandburg wanted to use his "proletarian art" as a way "to make life possible to the proletariat."

Babbette Deutsch reviewed the book of poems in late October of 1928 for the *New York Herald Tribune*:

> One must group him, if at all, with those men who are struggling to realize this nation, to formulate, in some sort, the spirit of the country. The son of an immigrant, himself a laborer, a farmer, a soldier, a newspaperman,

he has lived on the prairie and in the city and knitted the America he
found there into the fibers of his being ... It is this rare dry humor that
chiefly distinguishes him from his great predecessor [Walt Whitman]—a
humor that is as peculiarly of his own place and age as the proverbs he
has lumped together in one section of *Good Morning, America.* (qtd. in
Marowski 346)

This is precisely what Sandburg wanted readers to discover in his art—a "strug-
gle to realize this nation, to formulate, in some sort, the spirit of the country."
And at the center of that struggle was an effort to make his art, with its tightly
injected cohesive message, reach "the People."

John Crawford also reviewed Sandburg's *Good Morning, America* in the
New York Evening Post and stated that "Sandburg intensifies and makes dra-
matic the everyday aspects of experience. These lyrics are whimsical impressions,
brusquely humorous salutations, wistful questionings, nature sketches, minor
epics in homespun philosophy, and emphatic 'yeas.'" (qtd. in Salwak 30)

Penelope Niven reminds us, though, that Sandburg's literary project was grow-
ing in complexity when she explains how the concluding poem in the book, "Many
Hats," has a unique vigor because of "the fusion of forces at work in Sandburg's
imagination—the movies, the folk music, the 'kid' stories, his travels with ears
awake to the American idiom, his saturation in American history" (Niven 468).

Already fifty-one in 1929, Sandburg was about to initiate what can be seen
in retrospect as another prolific decade, publishing in 1929, *Rootabaga Country*,
a one-volume edition of his two earlier children's books. That same year, he
published a biography of his brother-in-law, Edward Steichen, and titled it
Steichen the Photographer. In 1930 he published *Potato Face* and *Early Moon*,
the first a collection of short stories for children and the second a volume of
poetry for young children. In 1932, with the help of Paul Angle, he published
a biography of Abraham Lincoln's wife and titled the work *Mary Lincoln: Wife
and Widow.* His book-length poem *The People, Yes* appeared in 1936 and the
four-volume biography of Lincoln's later years—*Abraham Lincoln: The War
Years*—appeared in 1939.

This period of massive publishing and extensive touring and lecturing saw
the tide turning on Sandburg, though. Many of his leftist supporters now
accused him of "becoming too commercial to be taken seriously as a man of
letters" (Niven 476). And yet, with absolute commitment, he continued to write,
to lecture, and to spread his working man's ideology.

Chapter 12

The People, Yes: *A Case Study of the Ongoing Labor Problem in the United States*

The People, *Yes* was published in October of 1936. The nation found itself "locked in a full-scale depression that did not bottom out until 1933 and whose effects lingered throughout the decade" (Boyer 870). Franklin D. Roosevelt had been in office since 1932, and to counter the cataclysmic horrors of the Great Depression, he had made aggressive efforts to propose and implement an array of emergency measures in his early months of office. Building on the optimistic tone of Roosevelt's Inaugural Address, Sandburg, an ardent supporter of Roosevelt, published *The People, Yes* at a time when the country was slowly rebounding from a crippled economy and a crippled national spirit. In addition, the Great Depression created even greater animosity between the rich and the poor. Historian Paul Boyer explains how "the 1929 crash had produced a bitter reaction against business executives" and also argues that "the financier, a hero of the 1920s business culture, seemed less awe-inspiring in the political climate of 1933" (Boyer 881).

The People, Yes was published in the midst of the New Deal at high tide. According to the anonymous *Time* magazine review, Sandburg's *The People, Yes* makes "the People," personified and acting as a collective unit, "a hero worth's a poet's tribute" (qtd. in Salwak 43). Archibald MacLeish, who consistently championed Sandburg's works, said of the book in the *New Masses*:

> Every radical should read this to learn that there is a living American tradition upon which a social revolution might be built. Our great tradition is a belief in people. A revolutionary party will achieve a people's state only by convincing the people of its belief in this tradition. (qtd. in Salwak 45)

MacLeish's comments are both accurate and insightful, and a close reading of *The People, Yes* reveals that many poems, indeed, not only show Sandburg's optimism in "the People," but they also aim at the possibility of a social revolution.

William Rose Benét said that "interesting as parts of it [*The People, Yes*] are, it does not think through, as does the modern radical economist, the situation in which modern civilization finds itself" (qtd. in Marowski 347). Stephen Vincent Benét described the book as one that

> is not dogmatic and it turns corners and goes around alleys. It is full of proverbs, questions, memoranda, folklore, faces and wonderings. It is a fresco and a field of grass and a man listening quietly to all the common-place, extraordinary things that people say. Yet it has its own coherence and its own confidence. (qtd. in Marowski 348)

About the text itself, Carl Sandburg wrote to fellow journalist Henry Luce, a communications tycoon, in early July of 1936:

> The book arose out of the monstrous efforts at debauching the public mind, which have gone on with increased intensity the past three years. I salute you on having had no hand in it ... But too many have luxuriated in the power of their rostrums, petted their passions, wreaked their whims. They think the people lap it up and everything is as it always was. Their conception of the public, the circulation, the audience, does not run with mine as I have presented in *The People, Yes*. They can't monkey with the public mind as they do without consequences. To bewilder a public with lies, half lies, texts torn from contexts, and then have that public sober and well-ordered in its processes, is not in the cards. (qtd. in Mitgang 343)

"The People" will live on, and even though they may be duped once or twice, they will eventually catch on, and once they do, "consequences" will follow. Sandburg concludes Poem sixty-two of *The People, Yes* by writing:

> The people laugh, yes, the people laugh.
> They have to in order to live and survive under lying politicians, lying labor skates, lying racketeers of business, lying newspapers, lying ads.
> The people laugh even at lies that cost them toil and bloody exactions
> For a long time the people may laugh, until a day when the laughter changes key and tone and has something it didn't have.
> Then there is a scurrying and a noise of discussion and an asking of the question what is it the people want.
> Then there is the pretense of giving the people what they want, with jokers, trick clauses, delays and continuances, with lawyers and fixers, playboys and ventriloquists, bigtime promises.
> Time goes by and the gains are small for the years go slow, the people go slow, yet the gains can be counted and laughter of the people foretokening revolt carries fear to those who wonder how far it will go and where to block it. (*The People, Yes* 158)

This statement directly echoes MacLeish's comment about the book's aim—one of social and class revolution, however gradual. Sandburg's "People" are intelligent and independent, and though they may be duped sometimes, they still possess a powerful collective force that, when ignited, can, and will, lead to radical social change.

A close examination of *The People, Yes* reveals that this work is a hard-hitting indictment of America and the problems created by economic disparity. These poems strongly resemble those in *Chicago Poems*, in that a significant number of them are angry and show a profound and pronounced bitterness, but these poems are even more militant, and overall there is a cohesiveness in this volume that does not appear in *Chicago Poems*. This is the reason Archibald MacLeish praised *The People, Yes* so highly in *The New Masses*. Poem 89, for example, is a damning and exhaustive study of how money corrupts some people—others it haunts; and for others, it generates a feeling of guilt that makes them use their money to benefit all mankind.

In Poem 89 Sandburg criticizes Marshall Field "for stipulating in a clause of his will/a fund of $25,000 be set aside and its income be devoted/to the upkeep of his tomb" (*The People, Yes* 228). But he praises

> That professor at the University of Wisconsin, working out a butter-fat
>   milk tester
> Good for a million dollars if he wanted a patent with sales and royalties
> And he whistled softly and in dulcet tone: What in God's name do I want
>   with a million dollars?
> Whistling as though instead of his owning the million it would own him.
>   (229)

Throughout the poem, Sandburg praises those entrepreneurs and individuals whose passion for their work superceded the goal of acquiring profits from that work. He also offers some memorable and didactic lines:

> "There are no pockets in the shroud" may be carried farther.
> "The dead hold in their clenched hands only that which they have given
>   away." (232)

Sandburg then concludes the poem:

> Why was this money wished on me merely because I was born where I
> couldn't help being born so that I don't have to work while a lot of people
> work for me and I can follow the races, yacht, play horse polo, chase if I so

> choose any little international chippie that takes my eye, eat nightingale
> tongues, buy sea islands or herds of elephants or trained fleas, or go to
> Zanzibar, to Timbuctoo, to the mountains of the moon, and never work
> an hour or a day and when I come back I find a lot of people working for
> me because I was born where I couldn't help being born? (233)

These poems represent a departure from those found in *Good Morning, America*. There are no landscape studies and no ruminations; nothing, including the day-to-day lives of the common man, is romanticized. Also, Sandburg often offers portrayals of the wealthiest in society, underscoring the artificiality of the life of the upper class and reminding us of how the common people labor endlessly to support the wasteful and unnecessarily extravagant lifestyle of the wealthiest in society.

In Poem 83 of *The People, Yes* Sandburg explores and attempts to articulate the duty of "Socialist art":

> Who can make a poem of the depths of weariness bringing meaning to
> those never in depths?
> Those who order what they please when they choose to have it—can
> they understand the many down under
> who come home to their wives and children at night and night after night
> as yet too brave and unbroken to say, "I ache all over"?
> How can a poem deal with production cost and leave out definite
> misery paying a permanent price in shattered health and early old age?
> When will the efficiency engineers and poets get together on a
> program?
> Will that be a cold day? Will that be a special hour? (212)

Sandburg clearly sees a disconnect between art and reality, art which leaves out "definite misery." Again, Sandburg's "Socialist art" aimed to bridge imagination and reality and to expose the inequalities he saw in the American capitalist system.

Other poems concern the dehumanizing working conditions of many Americans and show the role that the unions might yet play. In Poem 79, Sandburg writes:

> In Gloversville, New York, a woman daylong made mittens and the faster
> she made the mittens the more the wages coming in for her and her
> children.
> And her hands became like mittens she said,
> And in the winter when she looked out one night

Where the moon lighted a couple of evergreen trees:
"My God! I look at evergreens in the moonlight
    and what are they? A pair of mittens.
And what am I myself? Just a mitten.
Only one more mitten, that's all.
My God! If I live a little longer in that mitten factory the whole world will
    be just a lot of mittens to me
And at last I will be buried in a mitten and on my grave they will put up a
    mitten as a sign one more mitten is gone."
This was why she listened to the organizer of the glove and mitten work-
    ers' union; maybe the union could do something.
    She would fight in the union ranks and see if somehow they could
save her from seeing two evergreens at night in the moon as just another
pair of mitts. (204)

This poem is one of many that mentions strikes of one sort of another. It is also an effort to expose and highlight the dehumanizing effects of long and difficult labor on the lives of working Americans. This show of militancy is characteristic of *The People, Yes*, and Sandburg includes poems like these because he understands that direct action is the most effective way to solve social, political, and economic problems.

In toto, this volume of poetry not only centers on developing the theme of "the People," but it also contains many poems that make direct reference to specific tenets in the ideologies of the Socialist Party of America and the Industrial Workers of the World, ideologies Sandburg knew well. Ultimately, *The People, Yes* serves as a case study of the ongoing labor problem in this country. In Poem 38, Sandburg writes:

Have you seen men handed refusals till they begin to laugh at the
    notion of ever landing a job again?
Muttering with the laugh,
    "It's driving me nuts and the family too,"
Mumbling of hoodoos and jinx,
    fear of defeat creeping in their vitals—
Have you ever seen this?
    Or do you kid yourself with the fond soothing syrup of four words,
"Some men won't work"?
Of course some folks won't work—
They are sick or worn out or lazy
Or misled with the big idea the idle poor should imitate the idle rich.
[...]

What are the dramas of personal fate spilled over from industrial
    transitions?
What punishments handed bottom people who have wronged no man's
    house or things or person?
Stocks are property, yes.
Bonds are property, yes.
Machines, land, buildings, are property, yes.
A job is property, na nix, nah nah.
The rights of the property are guarded by ten thousand laws and
    fortresses.
The right of a man to live by his work—
    what is this right?
    and why does it clamor?
    and who can hush it so it will stay hushed?
    and why does it speak and though put down speak again
    with strengths out of the earth? (77)

This poem is one of many that attempts to underscore a problem plaguing the American economy, an economy that privileges and protects the wealthy and the things that often accompany wealth: stocks, bonds, machines, land, and buildings. Clearly, for Sandburg, the common laborer ranks as the lowest denominator in society, and his needs, even those needs essential to live, are ignored. Sandburg points out how "industrial transitions" often affect "the dramas of personal fate" for the common laborer.

In addition, *The People, Yes* also gleans the past as it examines the errors man makes. Poem 27 illustrates this perfectly:

In the folded and quiet yesterdays
Put down in the book of the past
Is a scrawl of scrawny thumbs
And a smudge of clutching fingers
And the breath of hanged men,
[...]
Of ears clipped, noses slit, fingers chopped
For the identification of vagrants,
Of loiterers and wanderers seared
"with a hot iron in the breast the mark V,"
Of violence as a motive lying deep
As the weather changes of the sea,
Of gang wars, tong wars, civil tumults,
Industrial strife, international mass murders,
Of agitators outlawed to live on thistles,

Of thongs for holding plainspoken men,
Of thought and speech being held a crime,
And a woman buried for saying,
"I listen to my Voices and obey them"
[...] (49)

This poem takes a look at the arbitrary force of those in power. The poem illustrates how, repeatedly, over the course of world history and American history, individuals are punished for speaking out and for questioning the status quo. But Sandburg confidently concludes the poem by writing:

"You may burn my flesh and bones and throw the ashes to the four
    winds," smiled one of them.
"Yet my voice shall linger on and in the years yet to come the young
    shall ask what was the idea for which you gave me death and what
    was I saying that I must die for what I said?" (50–51)

Early poems like this one frame the text. As a matter of fact, a close reading of the 107 poems reveals a pattern that begins with the first twenty-four poems serving as collections of epithets used by "the People." These poems are beautiful tributes to the common man. One such poem, and probably the most finely written poem in the volume, is Poem 9. In it, Sandburg describes a father's advice to his son, who is nearing manhood:

A father sees a son nearing manhood.
What shall he tell that son?
"Life is hard; be steel; be a rock."
And this might stand him for the storms and serve him for humdrum
    and monotony and guide him amid sudden betrayals and tighten him
    for slack moments.
"Life is a soft loam; be gentle; go easy."
And this too might serve him.
Brutes have been gentled where lashes failed.
The growth of a frail flower in a path up has sometimes shattered and
    split a rock.
A tough will counts. So does desire.
So does a rich soft wanting.
Without rich wanting nothing arrives.
Tell him too much money has killed men
and left them dead years before burial:
the quest of lucre beyond a few easy needs
has twisted good enough men

> sometimes into dry thwarted worms.
> Tell him time as a stuff can be wasted.
> [...] (18)

Here, not surprisingly, Sandburg injects a clear warning about the dangers of "too much money," and he concludes the poem with the father offering his son advice on the creative powers of solitude:

> Tell him to be alone often and get at himself
> and above all tell himself no lies about himself
> whatever the white lies and protective fronts
> he may use amongst other people.
> Tell him solitude is creative if he is strong
> and the final decisions are made in silent rooms.
> [...]
> Let him have lazy days seeking his deeper motives. (19)

The poem is saturated with words of wisdom, and not only is Sandburg encouraging readers to be wary of the evils of "too much money" he is also encouraging them to learn the value of solitude because of its "creative" potential. In many ways, this poem echoes Bill Haywood's goal of "making life possible to the proletariat" (Aaron 16).

Chapter 13

Remembrance Rock: *Retelling American History Through Narrative*

S andburg's final major literary work, published when he was almost seventy, was over four years in the making; it was begun soon after he published *Abraham Lincoln: The War Years,* which had earned him the Pulitzer Prize in History in 1940. The massive 1,100-page novel *Remembrance Rock* sold extremely well, but it received almost unanimously negative critical assessments. Even so, the novel was selected as a candidate for the Pulitzer Prize in Fiction, alongside James Gould Cozzens's *Guard of Honor,* Norman Mailer's *The Naked and the Dead,* Thornton Wilder's *The Ides of March,* Ross Lockridge's *Raintree Country,* and William Faulkner's *Intruder in the Dust* (Niven 589–90). (Cozzens received the Pulitzer.) Ultimately, the novel is a bold testament and confirmation of Sandburg's committed love for America, and in many ways the novel is written in the style of the two Lincoln biographies, but shows none of the rage that permeates *The People, Yes.* The novel articulates an optimism throughout its three sections, each of which can be seen as a separate and independent work. Book One is titled "The First Comers," and it is set in Plymouth Colony. Book Two, titled "The Arch Begins," is set during the American Revolution. Book Three, "The Arch Holds," focuses on the Civil War. The Epilogue, "Storm and Stars," is set at the end of World War II.

Lloyd Lews reviewed the book in the *New York Herald Tribune* on October 10, 1948 and said of it:

> *Remembrance Rock* is Carl Sandburg's ride to an American Canterbury—a long ride of 350 years with an American historical tale for every hoofbeat and an adventure for every garrulous pilgrim. Sandburg has with him in this, his first novel, many more riders than had Chaucer, and of these more are ploughmen and fewer are gentlemen and merchants, for Sandburg has been chiefly nourished on the speech and wisdom of the poor.

His method in *Remembrance Rock* is to create multitudinous characters, imaginary people who he feels, after years of research, are true not only to their respective periods in our national existence but to the whole American strain. They are the men who hit the beach at Plymouth in the 1600s and at Okinawa in the 1940s, who went underground to help George Washington in the 1700s and John Brown in the 1800s—the boys who shook, in turn, Cemetery Ridge and the hill of Cassino. His people are the farmers, clerks, housewives, private soldiers, hired girls; and if famous people like John Adams, George Washington, Abraham Lincoln, Myles Standish appear, it is only at a distance, with cornhuskers in fields and skillet-women around fireplaces talking of them.

... as a personal expression it is his fullest, ripest tribute to the dreamers and seekers who have followed "the blood-scarlet thread of America's destiny" that always stretches, as he says, into the Unknown—the people who have remained unswamped by fate and undulled by self-satisfaction. (qtd. in Marowski 351)

Sandburg opens the novel with a Prologue titled "Justice Windom's Box." In this chapter, readers are introduced to Justice Orville Brand Windom, a (fictional) former Justice of the United States Supreme Court, who was to give a "radio address to the American people. They had urged him that millions who knew his name and took him as a significant American figure would like to have coming into their homes his voice with a message for the time and hour" (*Remembrance Rock* 4–5). At this early point in the novel, America is in the fourth year of the Second World War, and Justice Windom offers a speech that reverberates with the central theme found in *The People, Yes.* That theme, prosaic though it may seem, is that the common people of this country are the ones who serve as the foundation and have fought to make this country what it is. Justice Windom says:

As I speak to you from the seclusion of my home, I can see many of your faces. They are the faces I have seen in our America, faces I have met from coast to coast, from the Great Lakes to the Gulf. They are the faces of today, of now, of this hour and this minute. Yet it is worth considering that many of those same faces have had their shining moments in our America of the past. We can go back fifty or a hundred years, two and three hundred years, and we meet these same faces of men, women and children. They shared in the making of America, in bringing this country on from the colonial wilderness days through one crisis after another. Their faces moved through shattering events and the heartbreak of war and revolution. Their faces gazed from the canvas slits of the covered wagon, from the glass windows of railway coaches, from the shatterproof glass of motorcars on concrete highways, from the Plexiglas nose of the latest make of airplane curving in the sky. They saw the years of startling change and dazzling invention, till America took her place among nations as one of the great world powers. In each time of storm, in each period of development, have been these faces—and I can see them out among you who are listening tonight. (19–20)

Once again, Sandburg presents his view of "the fate of man" as one of promise, and this conjecture is built on what he has seen in the past. Sandburg's novel crowds American history into 1,100 pages, for he believes that Americans living in the twentieth century can further solidify their view of where the country is headed by gleaning the country's past. For Sandburg, Americans should be "aware of the power of reality" (Straumann 142). And *Remembrance Rock* promotes this end; "it shows how their faces [those of the common people] have moved through shattering events and the heartbreak of war and revolution." The book offers a revisionist view of history. In essence, Carl Sandburg is retelling American history, and he makes it come to life, much like the Lincoln books made Lincoln come to life.

Book One, "The First Comers," recounts some of the earliest events in American history. It opens with a group of Englishmen, chiefly John Spong, his wife, and his daughter, Remember Spong, who in an effort to avoid religious persecution leave Scrooby Congregation in England and travel to Leyden, Holland. Eventually, the family, along with others, travel to America aboard the Mayflower, and in the Plymouth colony begin their lives. Hundreds of characters out of history appear in the course of the story line, including Roger Williams, William Bradford, and John Winthrop.

Throughout Book One, Remember Spong, the main character in this section of the novel, grows from a young girl of twelve to a young lady in her late twenties. In essence, Book One can be seen as a Bildungsroman of Remember Spong's journey to America and the life she led after her arrival, carefully chronicling her journey from childhood to adulthood. Her life story, though, is told against the broader outlines of American history. Sandburg pointedly reprints entries from William Bradford's journals, explains the development and purpose of the Mayflower Compact, and with neutral objectivity describes the first slaves brought to America. At every opportunity, he connects his characters to historical fact.

A typical passage that illustrates Sandburg's attention to historical precision and his strategy of adding to it a fictional spin can be found in chapter fourteen. There, Sandburg relates how Remember Spong always enjoyed visiting Elder Brewster (a fictional character) and his "more than four hundred books" (173).

Remember Spong and Elder Brewster discuss the importance of reading, but the discussion also makes an interesting comment about the danger of some books. Elder Brewster first explains to Remember about how the two hundred and eighty-one of the books had come

> over on the Mayflower. Since then more than a hundred other books had come on ships from England. He saw her hushed and awed before the array of volumes that marched along the bookshelves. The books stood still and seemed to say, "We can speak to you—open the covers and put your eyes on our letters and you will find we speak—we only seem to be silent."
> [...]
> "Wouldn't my head feel queer?" she asked Elder Brewster. "Wouldn't my head feel heavy carrying so much knowledge? Could any of it spill out if there was too much?"
> "No, my child. I have read all of them. Each writer of a book repeats himself. And they all repeat each other more or less."
> In each commentary, the Elder explained, the writer told what some part of the Bible meant to him. Another man searching the Bible for meanings might find such a book a help. As time passed there would be more commentaries written, till there were thousands. Then would come danger. A man might spend too much time reading the inquiries and discussions of others: he would then lose his own time for reading the Bible and searching his own heart many times over for the meanings. (173)

In this excerpt, we see a representative characteristic of the book: a commingling of fact and fiction. Sandburg carefully details some of the books the Pilgrims read. The precision and accuracy of Sandburg's list reveals the kind of care he gave to the preparation and writing of this book. Sandburg explains how while at Elder Brewster's home:

> She [Remember Spong] handled two volumes on civil government, *The Six Bookes of a Commonweale* by Knowles translated from *Les sez livres de la republique* by the French jurist Jean Bodin—and *Commonwealth of England and maner of Government thereof* by Sir Thomas Smith. A government in Plymouth she knew they had, and each year they elected a governor and a council. Now the thought struck her: there is government everywhere, either good or bad. And men who know about government write big bulging books about it.
> She held the volume *Two Bookes, of the proficience and advancement of Learning, divine and humane* by Lord Francis Bacon. Remember had heard him mentioned a few times: the man who had read and written more books than any other man in England. This crossed her mind. Elder

> Brewster smiled gravely. "Should you read it, you would find he desires men of learning should rehearse and revise their learning with more care. Their learning often is less deep and certain than they believe." (174 [italics in original])

This is the way the book moves. Factual and fictional characters appear in the novel as they confront the difficulties of beginning life in a new country.

An additional passage—again, one of literally hundreds—that shows Sandburg's attention to historical detail and accuracy appears in chapter fifteen when Sandburg describes life in Plymouth:

> The wide wild sea to the east, the treacherous thousand-mile wilderness to the west, their little huddle of houses stood as the first settlement on the coast of New England to stand up and stay put. Northward the French had forts in Canada. Southward the Dutch had trading posts, two hundred and seventy people and more than a hundred cattle, at the mouth of Hudson River and on Manhattan Island. Far down on the curving and jagged Atlantic coastline lay the Jamestown settlement. Who in Plymouth had not heard of death, starvation and ruin tracked across Jamestown and Virginia for twenty years? Shipmasters, seamen, officers of the crown, their vessels anchored in Plymouth Harbor, had their tales and reports of Jamestown. Across twenty years out of the ports of England, ships had carried more than five thousand and six hundred emigrants for Virginia. And hundreds had fled back to the old country, sick of hardship and terror. In single massacre three hundred and forty-seven men, women and children went down under the hatchets, knives and arrows of the Indians. Nearly one thousand died of sickness or want of food on the way to Virginia or in the colony. Its governor officially termed the year 1610 as the Starving Time. About one in five who had left England for Virginia was now alive and aboveground, the Virginia colony population numbering one thousand and ninety-five people—four out of five had fled or died. (200)

In every page, Sandburg's aim in this novel is to retell America's story—to make it come to life—and he privileges the history and the story of the country over any specific character. Again, American history furnishes the plot and is always in the foreground. Perhaps never before had America's history been transformed and come to life in such a way.

As Book One of the novel comes to a close, Remember Spong and Resolved Wayfare, the man she loves, discuss the inherent dangers of doing what custom dictates because "it is a stumbling block to truth" (316), and they reminisce on the reasons the Pilgrims left England: "Was it not because that old country was cruel and unjust and would not let them worship God as they chose? Did they not say they were leaving England for the reason that here they could in a new land, a hard and lonely land filled with savages, yet a new land and theirs to do with as they should order, here they would show the world what liberty of conscience, freedom of worship, could do?" (324).

Book Two, "The Arch Begins," presents the Winshore family as the main characters. It opens "on a March morning of the year 1775," in John Biddle's tavern in Philadelphia. The percolating sentiments about an impending Revolution are described in reprinted newspaper excerpts from the *Pennsylvania Gazette*. Colonists are bitter about discrepancies in their treatment, as we can see in this direct quote from the work:

In England	*In America*
1. A trial by jury of his country, in all cases of life and property.	1. A trial by jury only in some cases; subjected in others, to a single Judge, or a Board of Commisioners.
2. A trial where the offence was committed. [...]	2. A trial, if a Governour pleases, three thousand miles from the place where the offence was committed.
6. A free trade to all the world, except the East Indies. [...]	6. A trade only to such as Great Britian shall permit.
9. Freedom of debate and proceedings in their legislative	9. Assemblies dissolved, and their legislative power suspended, for the free exercise of their reason and judgment, in their legislative capacity. (370–1)

Sandburg describes how "year by year as more thousands of British troops had been poured into Boston, the struggle against them had taken many forms (395). Factual characters that come to life include Paul Revere, John Locke, Thomas Paine, Edmund Burke, and Samuel Adams, the American Revolutionary leader whose agitations spurred Bostonians toward rebellion against British occupation and rule. Also appearing in the novel are John Adams, George Washington, and Thomas Jefferson.

Concurrently, fictional characters like Ordway Winshore and Mary Burton discuss the meaning of the war and the meaning of America in chapter eighteen. Ordway Winshore says to Mary Burton:

> The face of America—who can read it? A few years ago it stood all wilderness. The First Comers plowed and hammered at the wilderness face of America and made it something else. Now those early strugglers are gone, their faces are vanished. Now along the east coastline nigh three million faces, add them up and get the sum total. Read that mass face, if you can. The good faces and the bad, the best faces of all and the worst, they make the face of America. Neither America itself nor the world across the wide wild sea can read this face—can tell the meaning of America. Look to any horizon where fog hangs heavy. There in that fog, clearing away into sunlight in the times to come, there you will find the face of America. (474–75)

Conversations like these are scattered throughout the book, and with these conversations we can see Sandburg's theme: America is a country that has struggled to develop its identity, and its pulse and heartbeat come from the common people that have participated in its development. Sandburg later adds that "The religious liberty to be seen in America foreshadowed farther and wider liberty" (529).

Essentially, Book Two explores the idea of "liberty," and characters throughout this section of the novel—part of a revolutionary society—are witnessing the forging of a new nation. In chapter twenty-six, the Winshores have a conversation with Jean Shepherd, who fell in love with Micheal McGillicuddy. He has left her to fight in the Revolutionary War, and they tell her that "Michael had gone to a great army fighting in a holy cause of human freedom, that if he died from fighting or camp fever it would be alongside some of the truest men that ever walked the earth" (560).

Sandburg describes the cost of freedom because he wants readers to understand what was required to forge a new nation.

Book Three, "The Arch Holds," describes the migration West and covers most of the nineteenth century, including the debate over the abolition of slavery. Some of the most important chapters discuss how

> another movement gaining more powerful headway had slowed down the temperance cause. There was a pledge Joel and Brooksany stood up

and spoke with the rest of the congregation as required of all members, the solemn promise to toil and advocate without ceasing to the end that slavery be recognized as a sin in the sight of God and that the duty, safety, and best interest of all concerned required its immediate abandonment, that the duty of every Christian was to proclaim that whoever holds his fellow man in bondage is guilty of a grievous wrong, that religion and justice teach that man cannot hold property in man. (648–49)

Sandburg presents the issue of slavery as the cornerstone issue of the nineteenth century, but he also describes how America blossomed into a powerful country during that century. In chapter five of Book Three, "Valley Forge and Wagons West," the character Brooksany's grandfather comments:

A new America is coming, sooner than we thought. The country is going to be more the other side of the Alleghenies than this side. A great new country, it will make changes we can't see now. A new people on a new land must have changes. They will make a new America. How they will do it my poor eyes can't see now. They will dig more canals and lay more railroads. Along the new water routes and railroads you will see cities big as Springfield, Boston, New York and Philadelphia, by God, bigger than London and Paris. (669)

As Book Three moves forward, the westward migration of the Winwold family continues, and one character they meet along the way explains how the goal "to carry Christian settlements, churches and colleges into the Empire of the New West, is a nobler theme for a classic and immortal epic" (714). The family eventually settles in the town of New Era, located up the Illinois River; the community grows with every passing year. In their

Presbyterian church they had heard the gentle Ralph Waldo Emerson, the crashing and angular Theodore Parker of Boston, and a score of the nation's famous speakers, writers, educators, ministers, who got off the five o'clock afternoon train from Chicago. And those men of the platform were all troubled and shaken over slavery, some of them trying to subdue a wrath they did not dare to explode in public. Each had his own affiliations, plans and measures related to what should be done immediately with slavery ... (733)

The characters in the novel engage in their own debate over the slavery issue as the major events in American history sweep past them, including "the case of Dred Scott [which declared] that slaves have not rights which the white man is bound to respect, that in law they are never thought or spoken of except as property, and that free Negroes whose ancestors were slaves cannot become citizens. Then in April, Baltimore & Ohio Railroad workers had given the country its first big railroad strike, with stubborn fighting of police guards over railroad property and troops called to put down riots" (801–02).

The characters in the novel (principally Omri Winwold and Mibs Wimbler) are given the opportunity to contemplate these issues. Sandburg also describes "The Winwold house [and] how it shook with the roar and surge of youth, of young America, [to] the coming of America" (827). Sandburg then discusses the issues and events that led up to the Civil War, and he has his characters speculating on the logistics of the war before it even begins (840). Surprisingly, Sandburg only spends four or five chapters on the Civil War, and he talks about the war only through the prism of how it affects a few characters in the novel.

There is no doubt that the novel is often overcramped and overcrowded with facts and characters, obscure historical information and documents, and is overloaded with facts and exhaustive lists. It concludes with an Epilogue that is set, once again, back in 1943, in the middle of World War II. Sandburg has his characters congregate around "Remembrance Rock"—a boulder that will serve as

> a place to come and remember. Here he [Justice Windom] had brought a handful of dust from Plymouth, Massachusetts, and here a colonial silver snuffbox filled with earth from Valley Forge, and here a small box of soil from Cemetery Ridge at Gettysburg, Pennsylvania, and here another handful of dust from the Argonne in France. As each man has his personal secrets, often whimsical and beyond explanation though deeply sacred, so it had been his decision many years back to spread around this Remembrance Rock and these four trees a small box of soil from Plymouth ... (5–6)

The novel shows Sandburg's "love of man in the huge collectivity of the American continent, and his sense of individual fates and surroundings, coupled with a unique and very personal feeling for the growth of his country" (Straumann 142).

The three central narratives in *Remembrance Rock* are intertwined in their aim and scope. Sandburg identifies three points in American history that could have led to a disintegration of the country and its people, but the people pushed through. The first settlers in Book One endured many hardships as they attempted to colonize this new country. Americans in 1776 fought for independence, and this led to tremendous industrial progress, which allowed America to enter a new age in the nineteenth century, which becomes the subject of Book Two. Finally, Book Three examines America in the period before, during, and after the Civil War, a war that radically divided the country.

What holds the novel together are the words of Roger Bacon:

> The Four Stumbling Blocks to Truth
> 1. The influence of fragile or unworthy authority.
> 2. Custom.
> 3. The imperfection of undisciplined senses.
> 4. Concealment of ignorance by ostentation of seeming wisdom.
> (*Remembrance Rock* 1066)

These four stumbling blocks appear in every section of the novel, and often the main characters contend with the meaning of these truths. Engraved on a bronze plaque, these words are passed down from one generation to the next. At the end of the work, we come to discover that all of these families are descendants of each other. In essence, then, this novel is the story of one family over four centuries.

There is perhaps more "unity of attitude in Sandburg's work than in most of the modern poets, in spite of the diversity of his writings" (Straumann 142). One unifying factor is his inclination to look deeply into America's history and its people. And from America and its people, he created a body of work that becomes Carl Sandburg's America—in it he highlights our achievements as a people and the promise that he sees. Common and ordinary people are the central characters of most of his work, and the potential they carry as a collective group is ever present.

1
2
3
4
5
6
7
8
9
10
11
12
13

Chapter 14

L iterary history has confirmed what Brian Reed points out in his article "Carl Sandburg's *The People, Yes,* Thirties, Modernism, and the Problem of Bad Political Poetry": "After 1951, Sandburg's academic reputation was calcified as the author of a handful of sincere but clumsy 1910s lyrics best appreciated by readers uneducated in subtleties of form, technique, and tone" (Reed 189).

Recovering Carl Sandburg is crucial to American literature. For too long, critical assessments have positioned him as a literary figure directly descended from Walt Whitman, which is a reductive over-simplification. Indeed, the two men shared a love for America and celebrated the common people in their works, but Sandburg's politics were vastly different from Whitman's. In addition, the America that Whitman saw in the second half of the nineteenth century was very different than the one Carl Sandburg saw in the first half of the twentieth century.

Other critical assessments compare Sandburg to Robert Frost, but Sandburg's literary project was altogether different. For Sandburg, the labor problem and the injustices—intentional or not—brought on by the creation of static socioeconomic classes became the most significant problem of the twentieth century. Beginning with *Chicago Poems* and in every work thereafter, he reveals himself to be a pragmatist as he responded to the problems that most deeply affected his countrymen. At the outset of his career, he wrote hard-hitting poems describing the abysmal working conditions of the working class, as seen in the first four volumes of poetry, but his literary project becomes much more exciting and much more complex after that period.

The only way to recover Sandburg from his current place as a marginal figure in American literature is by correctly assessing his use of a "new imagination," by fully examining his sustained effort at nation-building, and by understanding the political ideology present in virtually all his published works. This study is the beginning of that project. Scholars of American literature should recognize that "there is a greater unity of attitude in Sandburg's work than in most of the modern poets, in spite of the diversity of his writings" (Straumann 142). This unity, which William Carlos Williams and others saw as a weakness, should be reevaluated; Sandburg was a man of letters living in an age where the traditional role of the poet was changing. He offered new ways of reaching an audience, giving literally thousands of performances around the country from 1922 to 1950. This side of Sandburg—that of the poet as a performance artist—has also never been studied carefully enough.

Critical assessments of Sandburg become more accurate and complete when he is viewed contextually. We must remember that

> at the start of the twentieth century, intellectuals increasingly challenged the ideological foundations of a business-dominated social order, and writers and journalists publicized the human toll of industrialization. Soon reform thundered over the nation as activists sought to make government more democratic, eradicate unhealthful and dangerous conditions in cities and factories, and curb corporate power. (Boyer 760)

This was an age of historical revisionism, and Sandburg was actively participating in the period. This was the age of the Progressive Movement and the age of William James and his seminal work *Pragmatism*, published in 1907. James argued that

> truth emerges not from universal laws or abstract theorizing but from the stream of everyday experience, as we test our ideas in practice. Truth is what works. James's emphasis on the fluidity of knowledge and the importance of practical action contributed to the progressive mood of reformism and skepticism toward established ideologies. (qtd. in Boyer 762)

Early on, when he was a committed Socialist, Sandburg was, indeed, an ideologue, but by 1919 his many personal letters testify to the fact that he was a pragmatist. Sandburg realized the importance of "practical action"—and his live performances, in addition to his radio and television performances, all served that function. Tragically, for too long critical assessments of Sandburg have failed to see him this way. They still view him as a committed Socialist ideologue. Sadly, as Brian Reed points out, the books and articles that have been published on Sandburg over the last decade "display a pronounced bias toward a single phase in Sandburg's long career, the years 1915–1920" (Reed 186).

Indeed, the famous letter Sandburg wrote to Romain Rolland in October of 1919 echoes the pragmatism of William James:

> Until the earth is a free place to free men and women wanting first of all the right to work on a free earth there will be war, poverty, filth, slums, strikes, riots, and the hands of men red with the blood of other men. I am against all laws that the people are against and I respect no decisions of courts and judges which are rejected by the people ... Any steps, measures, methods or experiences that will help give the people this requisite strength and wisdom, I am for. I can not see where the people have ever won anything worth keeping and having but it cost something and I am willing to pay this cost as we go along—rather let the people suffer and be lean, sick, and dirty through the blunders of democracy than to be fat, clean, and happy under the efficient arrangements of autocrats, kaisers, kings, czars, whether feudal and dynastic or financial and industrial. ... (qtd. in Mitgang 170)

Like William James, Sandburg knew that "truth is what works." Sandburg said that he was "willing to pay this cost as we go along"—his literature and his commitment to his countrymen are proof of that.

Carl Sandburg should also be understood as a poet who was aiming to create a more harmonious country and an awareness of the innate interdependence between the different socioeconomic classes in American society in the twentieth century. And like John Dewey, whose *Democracy and Education* (1916) "argued that schools must not only teach the values of democracy and cooperation but embody those values through their methods and curriculum" (qtd. in Boyer 762), Sandburg's works aim to do the same.

The most recent major book-length study attempting to revive Carl Sandburg's literary reputation—*The Other Carl Sandburg* (1996)—was written by Philip R. Yannella. It is an extremely important book in Sandburg scholarship and served as the catalyst for this study. In his book, Yannella explores how Sandburg's early work as a journalist for the *Chicago Daily News* and his early poetry clearly reflect ties to the political ideology of the Socialist Party of America and the Industrial Workers of the World. Penelope Niven, in what has become the standard biography, *Carl Sandburg* (1991), anticipates Yannella, and like him, she believes that Sandburg's published works from 1908 to 1920 present a very clear political project that is deeply influenced by the ideology of these two labor organizations. Both authors assert that the four independently published volumes of poetry that appeared before 1916, as well as the three books of poetry published between 1916 and 1920—*Chicago Poems*,

Cornhuskers, and *Smoke and Steel*—reveal direct ties to the political ideology of the Socialist Party of America and the Industrial Workers of the World. But both authors believe that 1920 is the last year that reveals such ties. They argue that works published thereafter do not resound with the same ideological overtones. Specifically, in his Epilogue to *The Other Carl Sandburg*, Yannella says:

> If Mr. Sandburg wished to continue writing radical prose after 1920, and there is no evidence he did, he, like others, would have found publication possibilities severely limited ... That same reluctance to look back—or perhaps, to have his radical past impinge on his fame and good fortune— emerged in 1941, when he took great care to get some comments on his labor sympathies made in an appreciative study of his work "corrected." (Yannella 151, 155)

But a thorough examination of Sandburg's poetry and prose reveals that he did write radical literature, chiefly in *The People, Yes*.

As this study has shown, Carl Sandburg's life and massive literary output after 1920 not only reveal an important and significant continuity in his political agenda but an important broadening in its breadth and scope as well. Like the works published before 1920, his post-1920 works offer an extremely complex and fascinating political project, one that involves cross-pollinations and complex negotiations of different strands of Socialism, but is more pragmatic than faithful to the party line.

Ultimately, after 1920 Carl Sandburg's political ideology grew in scope, breadth, and complexity, though it remained consistent with its pre-1920 Leftist origins. But the point to be underscored is that always at the center of Sandburg's concerns was the "common man" and the "working people"—interchangeable terms representing the group of Americans that Sandburg wanted to serve. And with Sandburg there was always a conscientious and sustained commitment to present the problem of class struggle.

It is important to understand that Carl Sandburg is not alone among marginalized figures in American literature. As we have seen, much of the literature of the late nineteenth and early twentieth centuries explores the relationship between labor and capital, and it centers on exploring the misery in the lives of the "working class." The literature produced during this time period is a literature of analysis and protest, and the output on this subject by a wide range of authors is impressive. Though many writers offered compelling indictments of corporate greed and dehumanizing urban growth, interest in their work faded after the coming of the New Criticism. There is much work to do.

There is perhaps no better way to conclude this discussion than to quote Sandburg's concluding section of *The People, Yes*:

> The people will live on.
> The learning and blundering people will live on.
> They will be tricked and sold and again sold
> And go back to the nourishing earth for rootholds,
>   The people so peculiar in renewal and comeback,
>   You can't laugh off their capacity to take it.
> The mammoth rests between his cyclonic dramas.
> [...]
> The people know the salt of the sea and the strength of the winds lashing
>   the corners of the earth.
> The people will take the earth as a tomb of rest and a cradle of hope.
> Who else speaks for the Family of Man?
> They are in tune and step with constellations of the universal law.
> (284, 285)

Works Cited

Aaron, Daniel. *Writers on the Left: Episodes in American Literary Communism.* New York: Harcourt, Brace, and World, 1961.

Adler, Morimer J., gen ed. "Second Inaugural Address." *1858–1965: The Crisis of the Union.* Vol. 9 of *The Annals of America.* 18 vols. Chicago: Encyclopedia Britannica, 1968. 555–56.

Allen, Gay Wilson. "Carl Sandburg." *Pamphlets on American Writers.* Vol. 7. Minneapolis, U of Minnesota P, 1972.

Arenstein, J. D. "Carl Sandburg's Biblical Roots." ANQ 16.2 (2003): 54–60.

Basler, Roy. *The Lincoln Legend: A Study in Changing Conceptions.* Boston: Houghton Mifflin, 1935.

Baym, Nina, ed. *The Norton Anthology of American Literature.* 4th ed. Vol. 2. New York: W. W. Norton and Co., 1994.

Benson, Al. "'Honest' Abe's Biographer—Yet Another Socialist." *The Patriotist.* 13 July 2003. http://www.patriotist.com/abarch/ab20020225.htm.

Bernstein, Arnie, ed. *"The Movies Are": Carl Sandburg's Film Reviews and Essays, 1920–1928.* Chicago: Lake Claremont P, 2000.

Boyer, Paul S., ed. *The Enduring Vision: A History of the American People.* Vol. 2. Lexington: D. C. Heath, 1990. 2 vols.

Boynton, Percy H. "The Contemporary Scene: Criticism Revitalized." *Literature and American Life for Students of American Literature.* Boston: Ginn, 1936. 820–24.

Bradley, Sculley, and Harold W. Blodgett. *Leaves of Grass: Authoritative Texts, Prefaces, Whitman on His Art, Criticism.* New York: Norton, 1973.

Brogan, T. V .F., and Alex Preminger. *The New Princeton Encyclopedia of Poetry and Poetics.* Princeton: Princeton UP, 1993.

Brooks, Cleanth. *Modern Poetry and the Tradition.* Chapel Hill: U of North Carolina P, 1939.

Brooks, Cleanth, R., W. B. Lewis, and Robert Penn Warren. *American Literature: The Makers and the Making.* Shorter Ed. New York: St. Martin's P, 1974.

Callahan, North. *Carl Sandburg: His Life and Works.* University Park: Pennsylvania State UP, 1987.

Carruth, Hayden. "Sandburg's Middle West." *Nation* 24 Jan. 1953: 82. "Chapter Two: Lincoln Commemoration and the Creation and Development of the *Abraham Lincoln Birthplace* National Historic Site, 1865–1935." Abraham Lincoln Birthplace. National Park Service. 23 May 2005. http://www.nps.gov/abli/hrs2.htm.

Crawford, B. V., A. C. Kern, and M. H. Needleman. Outline *History of American Literature.* New York: Barnes and Noble, 1945.

Crowder, Richard. *Carl Sandburg.* New York: Twayne, 1964.

Cunliffe, Marcus, ed. *American Literature Since 1900.* Vol. 9 of *The Penguin History of Literature.* New York: Penguin Books, 1987.

Detzer, Karl. *Carl Sandburg: A Study in Personality and Background.* New York: Harcourt, 1941.

Dubofsky, Melvyn. *We Shall Be All: A History of the Industrial Workers of the World.* Abr. ed. Urbana: U of Illinois P, 2000.

Durand, Greg Loren. "The Cult of Lincoln." *America's Caesar: The Decline and Fall of Republican Government in the United States of America.* 23 May 2005. http://www.crownrights.com/blog/etext/cult_of_lincoln.htm.

Ellman, Richard, and Robert O'Clair, eds. *Modern Poems: A Norton Introduction.* 2nd ed. New York: W. W. Norton, 1989.

Ferguson, Margaret, Mary Jo Salter, and Jon Stallworthy, eds. *The Norton Anthology of Poetry.* Shorter 4th ed. New York: Norton, 1997. 1167.

Ferlazzo, Paul. "The Popular Writer, Professors, and the Making of a Reputation: The Case of Carl Sandburg." In *Mid America IV.* Ed. David D. Anderson. East Lansing: Midwestern, 1979.

Fetherling, Doug, and Dale Fetherling, eds. *Sandburg at the Movies: A Poet in the Silent Era, 1920–1927.* Metuchen, N. J.: Scarecrow, 1985.

Gold, Michael, Granville Hicks, Isadore Schneider, Joseph North, Paul Peters, et al, eds. *Proletarian Literature in the United States: An Anthology.* New York: International, 1935.

Golden, Harry. *Carl Sandburg.* Cleveland: World, 1961.

Greene, Sally. "'Things Money Cannot Buy': Carl Sandburg's Tribute to Virginia Woolf." *Journal of Modern Literature* 24.2 (2001): 291–308.

Hillquit, Morris. *The Double Edge of Labor's Sword.* New York: Arno, 1971.

Hoffman, Daniel. "'Moonlight Dries No Mittens': Carl Sandburg Reconsidered." *Library of Congress Quarterly* 36 (1979): 4–17.

Johansen, J. G. "They Will Say." *Explicator* 59.3 (2001): 134–138.

Jones, Peter. "Carl Sandburg, 1878–1967." *Reader's Guide to Fifty American Poets.* New York: Barnes & Noble, 1980.

Lee, Muna. "Reviews." *Double Dealer* 5 Jan. 1923: 38.

Lewisohn, Ludwig. *Expressions in America.* New York: Harper, 1932.

—. *The Story of American Literature.* New York: Harper, 1937.

Lowell, Amy. "Edgar Lee Masters and Carl Sandburg." *Tendencies in Modern American Poetry.* New York: Macmillan, 1917. 200–232.

Mace, Ronald. *Carl Sandburg's Lincoln: The Prairie Years, a Critical Commentary.* New York: Monarch, 1966.

Marowski, Daniel G., ed. *Contemporary Literary Criticism.* Vol. 35. Detroit: Gale, 1985. 337–360.

Millett, Fred B. *Contemporary American Authors.* New York: Harcourt, Brace, 1940.

Mitgang, Herbert, ed. *The Letters of Carl Sandburg.* San Diego: Harcourt Brace Jovanovich, 1988.

Modern American Poetry. "'Sandburg's Journalism': Haywood of the I.W.W." 10 Apr. 2004. http://www.english.uiuc.edu/maps/poets/s_z/sandburg/journalism.htm.

Murphy, James F. *The Proletarian Movement: The Controversy Over Leftism in Literature.* Urbana: U of Illinois P, 1991.

Mussey, Mabel H. B. "Books for the Younger Reader." *Nation* 6 Dec. 1922: 618.

Neely, Mark E., Jr. "Carl Sandburg." *Dictionary of Literary Biography.* Vol. 17. Detroit: Gale Research, 1983. 378–82.

Nelson, Cary. "The Diversity of American Poetry." *Columbia Literary History of the United States.* Ed. Emory Elliot. New York: Columbia UP, 1988. 913–36.

Nicolay, John G., and John Hay. *Abraham Lincoln: A History.* Ed. Paul M. Angle. Abr. ed. Chicago: U of Chicago P, 1966.

Niven, Penelope. *Carl Sandburg: A Biography.* New York: Charles Scribner's Sons, 1991.

Pattee, Fred Lewis. *The New American Literature: 1890–1930.* New York: Century, 1930.

Pearce, Roy Harvey. *The Continuity of American Poetry.* Princeton: Princeton UP, 1961.

Reed, Brian M. "Carl Sandburg's *The People, Yes,* Thirties, Modernism, and the Problem of Bad Political Poetry." *Texas Studies in Language and Literature* 46.2 (2004): 181–212.

Robbins, Harry Wolcott, and William Harold Coleman. *Western World Literature.* New York: Macmillan, 1938.

Rosenfeld, M. S. *The Modern Poets.* New York: Oxford UP, 1960. 155–56.

Rubin, Louis D. Jr. "Not to Forget Carl Sandburg. ... " *Sewanee Review* 85 (977): 181–89.

Salwak, Dale. *Carl Sandburg: A Reference Guide.* Boston, G. K. Hall and Co., 1988.

Sandburg, Carl. *Abe Lincoln Grows Up.* New York: Harcourt, Brace, 1928.

—. *Abraham Lincoln: The Prairie Years.* 2 vols. New York: Harcourt, Brace, 1926.

—. *Abraham Lincoln: The Prairie Years and the War Years.* One vol. ed. New York: Harcourt, Brace and Company, 1954.

—. *Abraham Lincoln: The Prairie Years and the War Years.* Reader's Digest Illustrated ed. Pleasantville, NY: Reader's Digest Association Ltd., 1954.

—. *Abraham Lincoln: The War Years.* 4 vols. New York: Harcourt, Brace, 1939.

—. *Always the Young Strangers.* New York: Harcourt, Brace, 1953.

—. *The American Songbag.* New York: Harcourt, Brace, 1990.

—. *Chicago Poems.* New York: Henry Holt, 1916.

—. *The Chicago Race Riots, July, 1919.* New York: Harcourt, Brace, and World, 1969.

—. *Complete Poems of Carl Sandburg.* San Diego: Harcourt Brace Jovanovich, 1970.

—. *Cornhuskers.* New York: Henry Holt, 1918.

—. *Early Moon.* New York: Harcourt, Brace, 1930.

—. *Good Morning, America.* New York: Harcourt, Brace, 1928.

—. *The New American Songbag.* New York: Broadcast Music, 1950.

—. *The People, Yes.* New York: Harcourt, Brace, 1936.

—. *Potato Face.* New York: Harcourt, Brace, 1930.

—. *Remembrance Rock.* New York: Harcourt, Brace, 1948.

—. *Rootabaga Country.* New York: Harcourt, Brace, 1929.

—. *Rootabaga Pigeons.* New York: Harcourt, Brace, 1923.

—. *Rootabaga Stories.* New York: Harcourt, Brace, 1922.

—. *The Sandburg Range.* New York: Harcourt, Brace, 1957.

—. *Slabs of the Sunburnt West.* New York: Harcourt, Brace, 1920.

—. *Smoke and Steel.* New York: Harcourt, Brace, and Howe, 1920.

—. *Steichen the Photographer.* New York: Harcourt, Brace, 1929.

Sandburg, Carl, and Paul M. Angle. *Mary Lincoln: Wife and Widow.* New York: Harcourt, Brace, 1932.

Sandburg, Charles A. *In Reckless Ecstasy.* Galesburg, Asgard P, 1904.

Sherwood, Robert E. "When Lincoln Rode the Circuit." *New York Times Book Review* 14 Feb. 1926: 1.

Shulman, Robert. *The Power of Political Art: The 1930s Literary Left Reconsidered.* Chapel Hill: U of North Carolina P, 2000.

Sorensen, Summer. "Poets New and Old: Reviews of Ammons and Sandburg." *Discourse: A Review of the Liberal Arts* 8 (Spring): 143–52.

Straumann, Heinrich. *American Literature in the Twentieth Century*. 3rd Rev. ed. New York: Harper and Row, 1965.

Tackach, James. *Lincoln's Moral Vision: Lincoln's Second Inaugural Address*. Jackson: UP of Mississippi, 2002.

Untermeyer, Louis. "Carl Sandburg." *The New Era in American Poetry*. New York: Henry Holt, 1920. 95–109.

—. *Modern American Poetry: A Critical Anthology*. New York: Harcourt, Brace 1936.

—. *The Pocket Book of Robert Frost's Poems: With an Introduction and Commentary by Louis Untermeyer*. New York: Washington Square P, 1977.

—. "Strong Timber." *The Dial* 65 (1918): 263–64.

Van Doren, Carl. "Flame and Slag: Carl Sandburg, Poet With Both Fists." *Century* 106 (1923): 786–92.

—. *The Literary Works of Abraham Lincoln*. New York: The P of the Readers Club, 1942.

Van Doren, Carl C., and Mark Van Doren. "Sandburg 1878—." *American and British Literature Since 1890*. Rev. ed. New York: D. Appleton-Century, 1939. 32–37.

Van Wienen, Mark. "Taming the Socialist: Carl Sandburg's *Chicago Poems* and Its Critics." *American Literature* 63.1 (March, 1991): 89–103.

Weirick, Bruce. *From Whitman to Sandburg*. New York: Macmillan, 1924.

Wells, Henry W. "New America." *The American Way of Poetry*. Columbia Studies in American Culture. 13. New York: Columbia UP, 1943. 135–47.

Whitman, Walt. "A Backward Glance." *Complete Poetry and Selected Prose*. Ed. James E. Miller, Jr. Boston: Houghton Mifflin, 1959. 443–54.

Williams, Stanley Thomas. *The American Spirit in Letters*. New Haven: Yale UP, 1926.

Williams, William Carlos. "Carl Sandburg's *Complete Poems*." *Poetry* 78.6 (1951): 345–51.

—. *Selected Essays of William Carlos Williams*. New York: Random House, 1969.

Wilson, Edmund. *Patriotic Gore: Studies in the Literature of the American War*. New York: Oxford UP, 1962. 115–17.

Winger, Stewart. *Lincoln, Religion, and Romantic Cultural Politics*. Dekalb, IL: Northern Illinois UP, 2003.

Yannella, Philip R. *The Other Carl Sandburg*. Jackson: UP of Mississippi, 1996.

CREDITS

CPSIA information can be obtained
at www.ICGtesting.com
Printed in the USA
LVHW081931180120
643886LV00016B/48

9 781631 892097